Discovering Computers
— Fundamentals
Student Success Guide

Gary B. Shelly

Misty E. Vermaat

Contributing Authors

Susan L. Sebok

Steven M. Freund

COURSE TECHNOLOGY
CENGAGE Learning

SHELLY
CASHMAN
SERIES

Australia • Canada • Denmark • Japan • Mexico • New Zealand • Philippines • Puerto Rico • Singapore • South Africa • Spain • United Kingdom • United States

COURSE TECHNOLOGY
CENGAGE Learning

**Discovering Computers —
Fundamentals: Student Success Guide**
Gary B. Shelly, Misty E. Vermaat

Vice President, Career & Consulting: David Garza

Executive Editor: Kathleen McMahon

Associate Acquisitions Editor: Reed Curry

Associate Product Manager: Caitlin Womersley

Editorial Assistant: Sarah Ryan

Director of Marketing: Elisa Roberts

Senior Marketing Manager: Tristen Kendall

Marketing Coordinator: Michael Saver

Print Buyer: Julio Esperas

Content Project Manager: Matthew Hutchinson

Development Editor: Lyn Markowicz

Management Services: PreMediaGlobal

Interior Designer: Joel Sadagursky

Art Director: Jackie Bates

Text Design: Joel Sadagursky

Cover Design: Curio Press

Cover Photos: Tom Kates Photography

Illustrator: PreMediaGlobal

Compositor: PreMediaGlobal

Printer: RRD Jefferson City

For product information and technology assistance, contact us at
Cengage Learning Customer & Sales Support, 1-800-354-9706

For permission to use material from this text or product,
submit all requests online at **cengage.com/permissions**
Further permissions questions can be emailed to
permissionrequest@cengage.com

Library of Congress Control Number: 2012930422

ISBN-13: 978-1-133-59645-5

ISBN-10: 1-133-59645-2

Course Technology
20 Channel Center Street
Boston, MA 02210
USA

Cengage Learning is a leading provider of customized learning solutions with office locations around the globe, including Singapore, the United Kingdom, Australia, Mexico, Brazil, and Japan. Locate your local office at:
international.cengage.com/region

Cengage Learning products are represented in Canada by Nelson Education, Ltd.

Visit our website www.cengage.com/ct/shellycashman to share and gain ideas on our textbooks!

To learn more about Course Technology,
visit **www.cengage.com/coursetechnology**

Purchase any of our products at your local college store or at our preferred online store **www.CengageBrain.com**

Printed in the United States of America
1 2 3 4 5 6 18 17 16 15 14 13 12

Student Success Guide

Every student can be successful in classes utilizing *Discovering Computers — Fundamentals*. Establishing goals for what students want to achieve in the course and knowing how to best use the tools available in the textbook and in the Computer Concepts CourseMate will help every student succeed in this course.

This Student Success Guide can help students succeed in this course in the following ways:

Perform better on tests and quizzes

This guide points to content and resources in the textbook and in the Computer Concepts CourseMate to assist with learning key terms, studying important concepts, and reviewing essential material. The Chapter Study Guide focuses on the most important material in each chapter and challenges students to complete questions in the Study Guide, helping reinforce the concepts learned.

Enable retention of material and promote transference of knowledge

Each chapter is organized into several different general goals students might have for the course, like being an informed digital consumer, and categorizes the content and resources available in the textbook and in the Computer Concepts CourseMate to help students achieve those goals. The Chapter Study Guide in each chapter helps solidify and confirm that students understand the material presented.

Understand the relevance of this material

Computing and technology is everywhere. Learn about why this material matters in everyday life with the scenarios and thought-provoking questions at the beginning of each chapter that relate chapter content and resources to students' day-to-day life.

Keep current with technology

This guide presents ways for students to learn about the latest advances, changes, trends, breakthroughs, and products associated with computers, devices, and related technologies. Search phrases enable students to explore independently for information online.

Learn how to most effectively use the Computer Concepts CourseMate and WebTutor content

A comprehensive user guide demystifies the wealth of learning tools available on the Computer Concepts CourseMate and enables students to take advantage of all the Computer Concepts CourseMate has to offer learners. The WebTutor user guide will help students to best utilize the additional study tools available on WebTutor to maximize the learning experience.

New Learning Opportunities

New to the Computer Concepts CourseMate for *Discovering Computers* are three Web applications that can help student comprehension of the material when students are away from a computer. The Web applications available only via the Computer Concepts CourseMate are developed for use on smart phones, as well as on tablets, laptops, and desktop computers.

Improve retention of the chapter terms with the Flashcard Web application. Study for an exam by reviewing the major points in each chapter with the Study Guide Web application or with the Practice Test Web application that provides multiple choice quizzing.

Computer Concepts CourseMate enriches the *Discovering Computers — Fundamentals* learning experience. For more information about the Computer Concepts CourseMate see the Preface of the *Discovering Computers — Fundamentals: Your Interactive Guide to the Digital World* textbook for a Computer Concepts CourseMate walkthrough to learn more about the resources available on the Computer Concepts CourseMate for *Discovering Computers — Fundamentals*.

Like us on Facebook and follow us on Twitter

Facebook posts and Twitter tweets will enable students and instructors to keep up-to-date quickly and easily with relevant technology changes and events in the computing industry. Become part of the Shelly Cashman *Discovering Computers* community.

For Instructors A brand new testbank of questions for this edition of *Discovering Computers — Fundamentals* promotes problem-solving and critical thinking, rather than requiring students merely to memorize and repeat the content in each chapter. Questions that challenge students to *think* about answers before responding ultimately creates a more solid, meaningful exam and assessment of student understanding of the material. All questions in the testbank relate to the Chapter Study Guide in the Student Success Guide.

Table of Contents

Chapter 1

Introduction to Computers

Why Should I Learn About Computers?

"I use computers to do homework, search the Internet, check e-mail, play games, post updates on Facebook, talk on Skype, upload photos from my digital camera, sync music with my phone, and so much more! So, why am I in this class? What could I possibly learn?"

True, you may be familiar with some of the material in this chapter, but do you know . . .

"Why am I in this class?"

- How to protect yourself from identity theft? (p. 10, Ethics & Issues)
- Which game system you might use in physical therapy? (p. 18, Innovative Computing)
- What types of embedded computers you use every day? (pp. 19–20, Embedded Computers)
- What types of computerized equipment an airplane's pilot uses to transport you safely to a destination? (p. 28, Computer Usage @ Work)
- Which computer company sold more than five million units of a single phone model during just one quarter? (p. 29, Companies on the Cutting Edge)
- How to create a blog? (p. 34 and Computer Concepts CourseMate, Learn How To)
- What steps to perform on your computer to determine its speed, its processor, and the amount of RAM it contains? (Windows Exercises, Computer Concepts CourseMate)

For these answers and to discover much more information essential to this course, read Chapter 1 and visit the associated Computer Concepts CourseMate at www.cengagebrain.com.

Q & A

How can I meet one or more of these goals?

Make use of the goal's resources for each chapter in the book and you should meet that goal by the end of the course.

Customize Your Learning Experience

Adapt this book to meet your needs by determining your goal. Would you like to be an informed digital consumer? A productive technology user? A safe user, protected from the risks in a digital world? A competent digital citizen? A future entrepreneur or professional in a digital society?

Every chapter in this Student Success Guide identifies resources targeted toward each of these goals, along with criteria to verify you understand the resources' content. Resources may be located in the textbook, on the Computer Concepts CourseMate Web site, in the interactive eBook, and on the Web.

Informed Digital Consumer

Goal: I would like to understand the terminology used in Web or print advertisements that sell computers, mobile devices, and related technology, as well as the jargon used by sales associates in computer or electronics stores, so that I can make informed purchasing decisions.

Topic	Resource	Location	Now you should . . .
Computer Hardware Components	Text/Figures	pp. 4–7	Know the purpose of input devices, output devices, the system unit, storage devices, and communications devices
	Drag and Drop Figure 1-3	eBook p. 5 or CourseMate	Be able to identify images on the Web or in magazines that show common computer hardware components
Types of Software	Text/Figures	pp. 11–12	Know the difference between system and application software
Personal Computers	Text/Figures	pp. 15–16	Know the difference between desktop and notebook computers
Mobile Devices	Text/Figures	pp. 16–18	Know the functions of tablets, smart phones, e-book readers, portable media players, and digital cameras
Digital Cameras	Web Link	eBook p. 18 or CourseMate	Be able to identify the top point-and-shoot and SLR digital cameras, their features, and their current prices

Continued on next page

Continued from previous page

Topic	Resource	Location	Now you should . . .
Game Consoles	Text/Figure	p. 18	Know the types of game consoles
Apple	Text	p. 29	Be familiar with Apple's recent products and developments
	Link	eBook p. 29 or CourseMate	
Amazon	Text	p. 29	Be familiar with products and services available through Amazon
	Link	eBook p. 29 or CourseMate	
Learning About Your Computer	Windows Exercise	CourseMate	Know how to determine the processor type, speed, and amount of memory (RAM) on a Windows computer

Productive Technology User

Goal: I would like to learn ways that technology can benefit me at home, work, and school. I also would like to learn helpful techniques for using technology so that I can perform tasks more efficiently and be more productive in daily activities.

Topic	Resource	Location	Now you should . . .
Using the Internet	Text/Figures	pp. 8–10	Know why people use the Internet and the Web sites they use to share and interact with others
Most Visited Web Sites	FAQ Link	eBook p. 11, or Top Web Sites link, CourseMate	Know how to find widely used Web sites and how to determine any Web site's current ranking
Windows	Web Link	eBook p. 11 or CourseMate	Know how to access Microsoft's online tips and help for using Windows
	Labs	CourseMate	Be familiar with how to use the Windows interface
Installing and Running Programs	Text and FAQ	pp. 12–13	Understand the processes of installing a program and running an installed program
	Drag and Drop Figure 1-10	eBook p. 13 or CourseMate	
Embedded Computers	Text/Figure	pp. 19–20	Be familiar with everyday products that contain or could contain embedded computers
	Looking Ahead	p. 24	
	Link and Video	eBook p. 24 or CourseMate	
Home User	Text and FAQ	pp. 20–21	Know how technology can help home users
Mobile User	Text/Figure	pp. 22–23	Know how technology can help mobile users
Education	Text/Figure	pp. 24–25	Be able to identify ways people in education use computers
Finance	Text/Figure	p. 25	Know how people use computers to assist with finances
Government	Text/Figure	p. 25	Be familiar with services offered online through government agencies
Travel	Text/Figure	p. 27	Know how people use computers in travel or with travel arrangements
Using Input Devices	Labs	CourseMate	Know how to use a mouse and keyboard
Google Maps	Web Apps	CourseMate	Know how to use Google Maps to locate places and obtain directions

Safe User, Protected from the Risks in a Digital World

Goal: I would like to take measures to (1) protect my computers, devices, and data from loss, damage, or misuse; (2) minimize or prevent risks associated with using technology; and (3) minimize the environmental impact of using computers and related devices.

Topic	Resource	Location	Now you should . . .
Disadvantages of Using Computers	Text	p. 7	Know the risks associated with using computers
Green Computing	Text	p. 7	Know strategies that support green computing
	Web Link	eBook p. 7 or CourseMate	Know where to find the latest news related to green computing
Identify Theft and Phishing	Ethics & Issues	p. 10	Know the steps you can take to deter identity theft
	Video	eBook p. 10 or CourseMate	Describe ways to be safe from phishing attempts
E-Waste	Ethics & Issues	p. 14	Know the potential hazards of e-waste and issues with recycling efforts

Competent Digital Citizen

Goal: I would like to be knowledgeable and well-informed about computers, mobile devices, and related technology, so that I am digitally literate in my personal and professional use of digital devices.

Topic	Resource	Location	Now you should . . .
Digital Literacy	Text	p. 3	Know why computer, or digital, literacy is vital to success
How Computers Process Data into Information	Text/Figure	pp. 3–4	Be able to define the term, computer, and distinguish between data and information
	Figure 1-2 Animation	eBook p. 4	Be able to identify examples of data, processes, and information
Advantages of Using Computers	Text	p. 7	Know the benefits of using computers
Google History	FAQ Video	eBook p. 11 or CourseMate	Be familiar with technological developments from Google
Convergence	Text	p. 14	Be able to give examples of technological convergence
Categories of Computers	Drag and Drop Figure 1-12	eBook p. 15 or CourseMate	Be able to identify images on the Web or in magazines that show each category of computer
Science	Text/Figure	p. 26	Recognize how scientists' breakthroughs in technology assist society
	Figure 1-35 Video	eBook p. 26 or CourseMate	Understand the benefits of using camera pills for 3-D imaging
Bill Gates	Text	p. 29	Be familiar with Bill Gates's impact on the personal computer and gaming industries and on society
	Link and Video	eBook p. 29 or CourseMate	
History of Computers and Other Digital Devices	Text	pp. 37–54	Be familiar with milestones in the history of computers and other digital devices
	Video	eBook p. 37 or CourseMate	
	Video	At the Movies, CourseMate	

Future Entrepreneur or Professional in a Digital Society

Goal: As I ponder my future, I envision myself as an entrepreneur or skilled professional using technology to support my business endeavors or job responsibilities. Along the way, I may interact with a variety of computer professionals — or I may just become one myself!

Topic	Resource	Location	Now you should . . .
Sharing Resources	Text	p. 8	Know why a business shares network resources
Software Development	Text	p. 13	Be able to identify the role of a computer programmer in a business
Apple vs. PC	FAQ Link	eBook p. 15, or Personal Computer Sales link, CourseMate	Be familiar with the types of personal computers being used in industry today
Handheld Computers	Text	p. 17	Know how businesses use handheld computers
Servers, Mainframes, and Supercomputers	Text/Figures	p. 19	Know the purpose of servers, mainframes, and supercomputers, and their role in organizations
SOHO User	Text/Figure	p. 22	Know how technology can help small office/home office users
Power User	Text/Figure	p. 23	Know how technology can help power users
Enterprise User	Text/Figure	pp. 23–24	Know how technology can help an enterprise and its users
Health Care	Innovative Computing	p. 18	Understand how game consoles are used in the medical field to assist professionals and patients
	Link and Video	eBook p. 18 or CourseMate	
	Text/Figure	pp. 25–26	Understand how technology assists medical professionals
Publishing	Text/Figure	p. 27	Understand how publishers use technology
Manufacturing	Text/Figure	p. 27	Understand how the manufacturing industry uses computers
Transportation	Computer Usage @ Work	p. 28	Know how professionals in the transportation industry use computers to support their activities
	Link and Video	eBook p. 28 or CourseMate	
Personal Computer Salesperson	Exploring Computer Careers	CourseMate	Be familiar with the responsibilities of and education required for a personal computer salesperson
Create and Use Your Own Blog	Learn How To	p. 34 and CourseMate	Understand the benefits of blogs to business owners; know how to create a blog and format it for display on a mobile device

Preparing for a Test

Visit the Computer Concepts CourseMate at www.cengagebrain.com and then navigate to the Chapter 1 Web Apps resource for this book to prepare for your test.

Does your class use the Computer Concepts CourseMate Web site? If so, prepare for your test by using the Flash Cards, Study Guide, and Practice Test Web apps — available for your smart phone or tablet.

If your class does not use the Computer Concepts CourseMate Web site or you prefer to use your book, you can prepare for the test by doing the Quiz Yourself activities on pages 8, 14, and 28; reading the Chapter Review on pages 30–31; ensuring you know the definitions for the terms on page 31; and completing the Checkpoint exercises on page 32. You also should know the material identified in the Chapter 1 Study Guide that follows.

Chapter 1 Study Guide

This study guide identifies material you should know for the Chapter 1 exam. You may want to write the answers in a notebook, enter them on your digital device, record them into a phone, or highlight them in your book. Choose whichever method helps you remember the best.

1. Define computer literacy, or digital literacy, and describe how its requirements change.

2. Define the term, computer.

3. Differentiate between data and information. Give an example of each.

4. Identify the activities in the information processing cycle.

5. Define the term, hardware. Give examples.

6. Describe the purpose of each of the five components of a computer: input devices, output devices, system unit, storage devices, and communications devices.

7. Identify examples of commonly used input devices, output devices, and storage devices.

8. The two main components on the motherboard are the _____ and _____.

9. List and describe five different advantages of using computers.

10. List and describe five different disadvantages of using computers.

11. Define the term, green computing. Describe strategies that support green computing.

12. Define the terms, network and online.

13. List two benefits of sharing resources on a network. Identify four types of resources that can be shared on a network.

14. Define the term, Internet. Identify reasons people use the Internet.

15. Differentiate between a Web page and a Web site.

16. Understand how phishing can lead to identity theft. Identify three ways to deter identity theft.

17. Explain the purpose of a social networking Web site.

18. Define the term, blog. _____ is a popular microblog.

19. Define the term, podcast.

20. Define the term, Web application. Give some examples of software available as Web applications.

21. Name three characteristics that classify a Web site as Web 2.0.

22. FAQ stands for _____.

23. Define the term, software, and then give a synonym for this term. Identify where you can obtain software.

24. Describe the characteristics of a graphical user interface.

25. Differentiate between system software and application software.

26. Microsoft's personal computer operating system is called _____. Apple's is called _____.

27. Distinguish between installing a program and running a program. Describe how to determine if software will run on a computer.

28. Define the term, programmer. A computer programmer may be called a _____. Name some programming languages.

29. Know the categories of computers. Give examples of convergence, with respect to technology.

30. Identify reasons e-waste can be hazardous and issues with recycling efforts.

31. List the components of a personal computer. Identify two popular architectures.

32. Differentiate between a desktop computer and a notebook computer. Notebook computers are also known as _____ computers.

33. Describe a digital tablet, or tablet computer.

34. Describe the purpose of these mobile devices: smart phone, PDA, e-book reader, handheld computer, portable media player, and digital camera.

35. Differentiate among a text message, picture message, and video message.

Continued on next page

Continued from previous page

36. Describe the purpose of earbuds.

37. Distinguish between a standard game console and a handheld game console. Identify popular models of game consoles. Explain how the medical field uses the Wii game console.

38. Differentiate among a server, mainframe, and supercomputer.

39. Define the term, embedded computer. Give examples of products that contain embedded computers.

40. Name the five categories of users and describe how each uses technology.

41. Describe how technology is used in education, finance, government, health care, science, publishing, travel, manufacturing, and transportation.

42. Identify Apple's tablet, portable media player, smart phone, and its online music store.

43. Amazon's e-reader is called the _____.

44. Bill Gates founded _____.

45. Technology milestones: Who was Dr. Grace Hopper? Who built the first Apple computer? When did the IBM PC enter the personal computer marketplace? Who invented the World Wide Web? Which online company started as a bookstore? Which online social network was originally available only to college students? When did federal law require all full-power television stations broadcast only in digital format? What was the benefit of HTML5?

Check This Out

As technology changes, you must keep up with updates, new products, breakthroughs, and recent advances to remain digitally literate. The list below identifies topics related to this chapter that you should explore to keep current. In parentheses beside each topic, you will find a search term to help begin your research using a search engine, such as Google.

1. **popular Web applications** (search for: Web apps)

2. **widely used Web sites** (search for: best Web sites, or popular Web sites)

3. **latest version of the Windows operating system** (search for: Microsoft Windows versions)

4. **latest version of the Mac OS operating system** (search for: Apple Mac OS versions)

5. **latest version of the iPad and iPhone operating system** (search for: iOS version)

6. **latest version of the Android operating system** (search for: Android version)

7. **widely used apps for tablets** (search for: best tablet apps)

8. **widely used apps for smart phones** (search for: best phone apps)

9. **latest models of e-book readers** (search for: e-reader reviews)

10. **features of popular portable media players** (search for: portable media player features)

11. **widely used digital cameras** (search for: popular digital cameras)

12. **popular Xbox 360 games** (search for: top Xbox games)

13. **popular Wii games** (search for: top Wii games)

14. **popular PlayStation games** (search for: top PlayStation games)

15. **widely used travel Web sites** (search for: popular travel Web sites)

For current news and information
Check us out on Facebook and Twitter. See your instructor or the Computer Concepts CourseMate for specific information.

Chapter 2

The Internet and the World Wide Web

Why Should I Learn About the Internet and the Web?

"I use the Internet and Web to shop for bargains, browse Google for all sorts of information, manage my fantasy sports teams, download music from iTunes, check e-mail on my phone, and so much more! Really, what more could I gain from the Internet or the Web?"

True, you may be familiar with some of the material in this chapter, but do you know . . .

"What more could I gain from the Internet or the Web?"

- Why you might support a do-not-track list? (p. 65, Ethics & Issues)
- Where you can obtain free plug-ins? (p. 73, Figure 2-15)
- How to create and publish your own Web page? (p. 74 and Computer Concepts CourseMate)
- If you follow the code of acceptable behavior for online activities? (p. 81, Netiquette)
- How lighting technicians and audio engineers use computers to enhance your concert-going experiences? (p. 82, Computer Usage @ Work)
- How Mark Zuckerberg's college experiences led him to develop Facebook? (p. 83, Technology Trailblazers)
- How to search for a job online? (Student Edition Labs, Computer Concepts CourseMate)
- Which Web sites list job openings? (p. 105, Making Use of the Web Special Feature)

For these answers and to discover much more information essential to this course, read Chapter 2 and visit the associated Computer Concepts CourseMate at www.cengagebrain.com.

Q & A

How can I meet one or more of these goals?

Make use of the goal's resources for each chapter in the book and you should meet that goal by the end of the course.

Customize Your Learning Experience

Adapt this book to meet your needs by determining your goal. Would you like to be an informed digital consumer? A productive technology user? A safe user, protected from the risks in a digital world? A competent digital citizen? A future entrepreneur or professional in a digital society?

Every chapter in this Student Success Guide identifies resources targeted toward each of these goals, along with criteria to verify you understand the resources' content. Resources may be located in the textbook, on the Computer Concepts CourseMate Web site, in the interactive eBook, and on the Web.

Informed Digital Consumer

Goal: I would like to understand the terminology used in Web or print advertisements that sell computers, mobile devices, and related technology, as well as the jargon used by sales associates in computer or electronics stores, so that I can make informed purchasing decisions.

Topic	Resource	Location	Now you should . . .
Broadband Internet Service and Providers	Text and FAQ	pp. 57–58	Know various high-speed alternatives for connecting to and accessing the Internet
	Labs	CourseMate	
Wireless Modems	Web Link	p. 58	Be able to identify various wireless modem options
Mobile Devices	FAQ Link	eBook p. 59, or Mobile Internet link, CourseMate	Be able to identify top mobile devices and accessories
E-Commerce	Text	pp. 74–75	Know how to shop online or how an online auction works
Cartoon Animation Software	Video	eBook p. 82 or CourseMate	Be familiar with software that animates artwork
eBay	Text	p. 83	Be familiar with services offered by eBay
	Link	eBook p. 83 or CourseMate	

Productive Technology User

Goal: I would like to learn ways that technology can benefit me at home, work, and school. I also would like to learn helpful techniques for using technology so that I can perform tasks more efficiently and be more productive in daily activities.

Topic	Resource	Location	Now you should . . .
Internet Addresses	Text	p. 60	Know components of IP addresses and their relationship to domain names
Internet Connections	Labs	CourseMate	Know how to connect to and disconnect from the Internet
Internet Properties and Internet Explorer	Windows Exercises	CourseMate	Know how to modify Internet properties, including browsing history, security settings, and privacy controls; and how to use Internet Explorer
Web Browsing	Text	pp. 61–62	Be able to use a Web browser
	Labs	CourseMate	
Web Addresses	Text	p. 63	Know how to enter a Web address in a browser
	Drag and Drop Figure 2-6	eBook p. 63 or CourseMate	Know the components of a Web address (URL)
Navigating Web Pages	Text	p. 64	Know how to use links to navigate Web pages
Tabbed Browsing	Web Link	eBook p. 64 or CourseMate	Be able to use tabbed browsing in Firefox
Searching the Web	Text	pp. 65–67	Know how to use search engines and subject directories
	Drag and Drop Figure 2-9	p. 66	
	Labs	CourseMate	
	Learn How To	pp. 88–89 and CourseMate	
Evaluating a Web Site	Text	p. 70	Know the seven criteria for evaluating a Web site
	Drag and Drop Figure 2-12	eBook p. 70 or CourseMate	
WorldWide Telescope	Innovative Computing	p. 71	Know how to use a computer as a telescope
	Link	eBook p. 71 or CourseMate	
Downloading Music	Text	p. 72	Know how to purchase, download, and listen to music
Web Video	Text and FAQ	p. 73	Know how to view video on a computer or device
Plug-Ins	Text	p. 73	Know the purpose of widely used plug-ins and where to download them
E-Mail	Text	pp. 75–77	Know various e-mail programs, and how to compose and send e-mail messages
	Figure 2-18 Animation	eBook p. 77 or CourseMate	
	Web Link	eBook p. 77 or CourseMate	
	Labs	CourseMate	
	Web Apps	CourseMate	
	Learn How To	p. 88 and CourseMate	
Instant Messaging	Text	pp. 78–79	Know how use instant messaging
Chat Rooms	Text	p. 79	Know how to use a chat room

Continued on next page

Continued from previous page

Topic	Resource	Location	Now you should . . .
VoIP	Text	p. 80	Know how VoIP works
FTP	Text	p. 80	Know how to use FTP
Newsgroups	Text	p. 80	Be familiar with newsgroups
Using Web Sites	Text	pp. 91–106	Be familiar with a variety of useful Web sites

Safe User, Protected from the Risks in a Digital World

Goal: I would like to take measures to (1) protect my computers, devices, and data from loss, damage, or misuse; (2) minimize or prevent risks associated with using technology; and (3) minimize the environmental impact of using computers and related devices.

Topic	Resource	Location	Now you should . . .
Web Site Tracking	Ethics & Issues	p. 65	Know issues with Web site tracking and online profiles
Using Wikis for Research	Ethics & Issues	p. 68	Describe the controversy surrounding using a wiki as a valid source of research
Online Payment Services	Text	p. 75	Be familiar with various online payment services designed to provide fraud protection
	Web Link	eBook p. 75 or CourseMate	
E-Mail Viruses	FAQ	p. 77	Recognize that viruses can spread through infected e-mail attachments
Cyberbullying	Ethics & Issues	p. 81	Know how to identify cyberbullying and recognize ways to protect yourself from it
	Video	eBook p. 81 or CourseMate	

Competent Digital Citizen

Goal: I would like to be knowledgeable and well-informed about computers, mobile devices, and related technology, so that I am digitally literate in my personal and professional use of digital devices.

Topic	Resource	Location	Now you should . . .
Evolution of the Internet	Text	pp. 56–57	Know how the Internet evolved to its present day form
W3C	Text	p. 57	Know the role of W3C with the Internet
Internet Backbone	Text	p. 59	Understand the basics of how data and information travel the Internet
	Drag and Drop Figure 2-2	eBook p. 59 or CourseMate	
Web and Web 2.0	Text	p. 61	Recognize Web pages and Web 2.0 sites
Web 3.0	Looking Ahead	p. 61	Understand the significance of Web 3.0
Web Site Types	Text	pp. 67–70	Know the purpose of various types of Web sites
Netiquette	Text	p. 81	Know the code of acceptable online behavior

Continued on next page

Continued from previous page

Topic	Resource	Location	Now you should . . .
Computers in Entertainment	Computer Usage @ Work	p. 82	Recognize how computers are used in music, movies, games, and performances
Google	Text	p. 83	Be familiar with Google's products and services
	Link	eBook p. 83 or Coursemate	
Tim Berners-Lee	Text	p. 83	Be familiar with the Internet and Web accomplishments and current endeavors of Tim Berners-Lee
	Link	eBook p. 83 or CourseMate	
Mark Zuckerburg	Text	p. 83	Be familiar with Mark Zuckerburg's impact on online social networks
	Link and Video	eBook p. 83 or CourseMate	

Future Entrepreneur or Professional in a Digital Society

Goal: As I ponder my future, I envision myself as an entrepreneur or skilled professional using technology to support my business endeavors or job responsibilities. Along the way, I may interact with a variety of computer professionals — or I may just become one myself!

Topic	Resource	Location	Now you should . . .
Popular Browsers	FAQ Link	eBook p. 61, or Browser Market Share link, CourseMate	Know the market share of browsers for desktop and mobile devices
Business/Marketing Web Sites	Text	p. 68	Know the purpose of a business Web site
RSS	Text	p. 70	Recognize why a business might push content to subscribers
Web Graphics Formats	Text	pp. 70–71	Know graphics formats for creating Web pages
Web Animation	Text	p. 71	Know the purpose of animation in Web pages
Web Audio - Formats and Distribution	Text	p. 72	Know an audio format compatible with Web pages, and various methods of distributing audio on a Web page
Virtual Reality	Text	p. 73	Know the purpose of virtual reality
Web Publishing	Text	p. 74	Know the steps to follow when developing and publishing a Web page
	Drag and Drop	p. 74	
Web Page Authoring	Web Link	eBook p. 74 or CourseMate	Know the tools developers use to create Web pages
Mailing Lists	Text	p. 78	Recognize why businesses use mailing lists
Video Blogs	Video	At the Movies, CourseMate	Know how to create and publish a video blog
Web Developer	Exploring Computer Careers	CourseMate	Be familiar with the responsibilities of and education required for a Web developer

Preparing for a Test

Visit the Computer Concepts CourseMate at www.cengagebrain.com and then navigate to the Chapter 2 Web Apps resource for this book to prepare for your test.

Does your class use the Computer Concepts CourseMate Web site? If so, prepare for your test by using the Flash Cards, Study Guide, and Practice Test Web apps — available for your smart phone or tablet.

If your class does not use the Computer Concepts CourseMate Web site or you prefer to use your book, you can prepare for the test by doing the Quiz Yourself activities on pages 61, 75, and 82; reading the Chapter Review on pages 84–85; ensuring you know the definitions for the terms on page 85; and completing the Checkpoint exercises on page 86. You also should know the material identified in the Chapter 2 Study Guide that follows.

Chapter 2 Study Guide

This study guide identifies material you should know for the Chapter 2 exam. You may want to write the answers in a notebook, enter them on your digital device, record them into a phone, or highlight them in your book. Choose whichever method helps you remember the best.

1. List the two goals of ARPANET. Name the year it became functional.

2. Describe the role of a host on a network.

3. Explain how ARPANET and hosts contributed to the evolution of the Internet.

4. Identify the role of the W3C.

5. Briefly describe seven types of broadband Internet service.

6. State the purpose of a hot spot. Name locations you might find one.

7. Define the term, access provider.

8. Differentiate among a regional ISP, a national ISP, an online service provider, and a wireless Internet service provider.

9. Major carriers of Internet traffic are known collectively as the Internet _____.

10. Describe the purpose and composition of an IP address.

11. Define the term, domain name. Cite an example of one.

12. Know the purpose of several generic TLDs.

13. Distinguish among the Web, a Web page, a Web site, and a Web server. Describe the role of each when a browser displays a home page.

14. Explain the purpose of a Web browser. Name five popular browsers for personal computers.

15. Define the terms, downloading and uploading.

16. Define the term, Web address. Name a synonym.

17. Name and give examples of the four components of a Web address. Identify the two components that may be optional.

18. State the purpose of a bookmark.

19. A _____ is a built-in connection to another related Web page or part of a Web page.

20. Describe what happens when you click a link.

21. Describe the function and purpose of tabbed browsing.

22. Differentiate between a search engine and a subject directory.

23. Besides Web pages, identify other types of items a search engine can find.

24. Describe how to use a search engine to search for information. Give an example of search text.

25. Describe ways to improve search results.

26. Describe the purpose of these types of Web sites: portal, news, informational, business/marketing, blog, wiki, online social network, educational, entertainment, advocacy, Web app, content aggregator, and personal.

27. Explain the controversy surrounding using a wiki as a valid source of research. Name a widely used wiki.

28. Describe seven criteria for evaluating a Web site's content.

29. Define the term, multimedia.

30. Explain how Web pages use graphics, animation, audio, video, virtual reality, and plug-ins.

31. Name the types of graphics formats used on the Web.

32. Define the term, thumbnail.

33. Name some popular audio file players.

34. Define the term, streaming. Identify uses of streaming audio.

35. Identify the purpose of popular plug-ins.

36. Identify and briefly describe the steps in Web publishing.

37. Define the term, e-commerce. Describe and give examples of the types of e-commerce: B2C, C2C, and B2B.

38. Describe the purpose of these Internet services and explain how each works: e-mail, mailing lists, instant messaging, chat rooms, VoIP, and FTP.

Continued on next page

Continued from previous page

39. _____ and _____ are two popular free e-mail Web apps.

40. Describe the components of an e-mail address.

41. Define the term, real time.

42. Define the term, netiquette. Identify the rules of netiquette.

43. Describe cyberbullying, how it occurs, and why it is difficult to catch the perpetrators.

44. Describe the purpose of these Web sites: Google, Webopedia, Blogger, Bloglines, Twitter, Facebook, LinkedIn, flickr, Shutterfly, YouTube, Expedia, Maps.com, E*TRADE, THOMAS, craigslist, eBay, Amazon, The Weather Channel, Yahoo! Sports, MSNBC, HowStuffWorks, NASA, WebMD, Monster, and Project Gutenberg.

Check This Out

As technology changes, you must keep up with updates, new products, breakthroughs, and recent advances to remain digitally literate. The list below identifies topics related to this chapter that you should explore to keep current. In parentheses beside each topic, you will find a search term to help begin your research using a search engine, such as Google.

For current news and information
Check us out on Facebook and Twitter. See your instructor or the Computer Concepts CourseMate for specific information.

1. standards that alert users to unauthorized Web tracking (search for: W3C Web tracking alerts)

2. broadband Internet service in rural areas (search for: extend broadband rural)

3. broadband upload and download speed tests (search for: broadband speed test)

4. new top-level domains (search for: top-level domain)

5. popular mobile Internet Web sites (search for: top mobile device sites)

6. today's most common search queries (search for: top search terms)

7. widely used online social networks (search for: online social networks)

8. errors found in Wikipedia (search for: Wikipedia mistakes)

9. computer games and game player statistics (search for: computer game industry statistics)

10. latest Web graphics formats (search for: latest Web image file types)

11. latest version of iTunes (search for: iTunes version)

12. recent uses of virtual reality (search for: virtual reality news)

13. latest news about cyberbullying (search for: cyberbullying laws)

14. latest music apps (search for: music apps)

15. popular weather Web sites (search for: weather sites)

Student Success Guide
Application Software

Why Should I Learn About Application Software?

"I use my computer mostly to type homework assignments, pay bills online, enhance digital photos, update my blog, and play games. Several years ago, a friend installed an antivirus program to protect my computer from viruses. What more software could I possibly need?"

True, you may be familiar with some of the material in this chapter, but do you know . . .

"What more
software could I
possibly need?"

- Which software can help you take notes? (p. 112, Figure 3-4, and p. 118)
- How fireworks shows use software to synchronize their displays with music? (p. 120, Innovative Computing)
- How CAD software helps architects and engineers design and construct buildings? (p. 121, Computer-Aided Design; p. 132, Computer Usage @ Work)
- Which software company is the largest? (p. 133, Companies on the Cutting Edge)
- How to zip a file? (pp. 138–139 and Computer Concepts CourseMate, Learn How To)
- How to use WordPad? (Windows Exercises, Computer Concepts CourseMate)
- Why texting can be harmful? (p. 144, Digital Communications Special Feature)

For these answers and to discover much more information essential to this course, read Chapter 3 and visit the associated Computer Concepts CourseMate at www.cengagebrain.com.

Q&A How can I meet one or more of these goals?

Make use of the goal's resources for each chapter in the book and you should meet that goal by the end of the course.

Customize Your Learning Experience

Adapt this book to meet your needs by determining your goal. Would you like to be an informed digital consumer? A productive technology user? A safe user, protected from the risks in a digital world? A competent digital citizen? A future entrepreneur or professional in a digital society?

Every chapter in this Student Success Guide identifies resources targeted toward each of these goals, along with criteria to verify you understand the resources' content. Resources may be located in the textbook, on the Computer Concepts CourseMate Web site, in the interactive eBook, and on the Web.

Informed Digital Consumer

Goal: I would like to understand the terminology used in Web or print advertisements that sell computers, mobile devices, and related technology, as well as the jargon used by sales associates in computer or electronics stores, so that I can make informed purchasing decisions.

Topic	Resource	Location	Now you should . . .
Software Availability	Text	pp. 108–109	Know the seven forms through which software is available
Business Software	Text/Figure	p. 112	Be able to identify widely used business programs
Business Software for Phones and PIM	Text	pp. 118–119	Know the types of business software available for phones and features of personal information manager software
Graphics and Multimedia	Text/Figure	p. 120	Be able to identify widely used graphics and multimedia software
Graphics Software	Web Link	eBook p. 120 or CourseMate	Be able to identify the top graphics software and supporting devices
Home, Personal, Educational Software	Text/Figure	p. 123	Be able to identify widely used programs for home/personal/ educational use

Continued on next page

Continued from previous page

Topic	Resource	Location	Now you should . . .
Adobe	Text	p. 133	Be familiar with Adobe's software
	Link	eBook p. 133 or CourseMate	
Microsoft	Text	p. 133	Be familiar with Microsoft's products and services
	Link and Video	eBook p. 133 or CourseMate	

Productive Technology User

Goal: I would like to learn ways that technology can benefit me at home, work, and school. I also would like to learn helpful techniques for using technology so that I can perform tasks more efficiently and be more productive in daily activities.

Topic	Resource	Location	Now you should . . .
Windows Programs	Text/Figure	pp. 110–111	Know Windows elements and how to start and use a program
	Drag and Drop Figure 3-3	p. 111	
Word Processing Software	Text/Figures	pp. 113–114	Know the features available in word processing software
	Web Link	eBook p. 114 or CourseMate	
	Ethics & Issues	p. 113	Know issues surrounding word processing use
	Labs, Windows Exercises	CourseMate	Be able to use word processing software
Developing a Document	Text/Figure	p. 114	Understand the tasks involved with creating, editing, formatting, saving, and printing documents
	Windows Exercises	CourseMate	Know how to create a document in WordPad and use its Help feature
	Learn How To	eBook pp. 138–139 or CourseMate	Know how to save a file and zip a file
Spreadsheet Software	Text/Figures	pp. 115–116	Know the organization of and features in spreadsheet software
	Labs	CourseMate	Be able to use spreadsheet software
Database Software	Text/Figure	pp. 116–117	Be able to describe a database, its organization, and how database software works
	Labs	CourseMate	Be able to use database software
Presentation Software	Text/Figure	p. 117	Know the features available in presentation software
Note Taking Software	Text/Figure	p. 118	Know the function of note taking software
Business Software Suite	Text	p. 118	Know the programs in and advantages of a business software suite; give examples
Document Mgmt.	Text/Figure	p. 119	Know the purpose of document management software and PDF files
Personal Finance	Text/Figure and FAQ	p. 124	Know the purpose of personal finance software
Legal Software	Text/Figure	p. 125	Know the benefits of using legal software and types of documents provided
Tax Preparation	Text/Figure	p. 125	Know the features of tax preparation software
DTP Software	Text/Figure	p. 125	Know the purpose of and how to use personal DTP software

Continued on next page

Continued from previous page

Topic	Resource	Location	Now you should . . .
Paint/Image/Photo Editing	Text/Figure	p. 126	Know the purpose and capabilities of personal paint/image editing and photo editing software
	Figure Video	eBook p. 126 or CourseMate	
Clip Art/Image Gallery	Text/Figure	p. 126	Know the benefits of clip art/image gallery software
Video and Audio Editing	Text/Figure	p. 126	Know the basic features of video and audio editing software
	Video	At the Movies, CourseMate	Know how to convert media files to a format for mobile devices
Design/Landscaping	Text/Figure	p. 127	Know the basic features of home design/landscaping software
Travel and Mapping	Text/Figure	p. 127	Know the benefits of using travel and mapping software
Reference	Text/Figure	p. 127	Know various types of reference and educational software
Web Apps	Text/Figures	pp. 128–129	Know the purpose of several Web apps
	Web Apps	CourseMate	Know how to use Britannica.com
Communications	Text/Figure	p. 130	Know the purpose of a variety of programs used for home and business communications
	Drag and Drop Figure 3-35	eBook p. 130 or CourseMate	
Help	Text/Figure	p. 131	Understand how to use online and Web-based Help
Digital Communications – Personal Use	Text/Figures	pp. 142, 144, 146, 148, 150, and 152	Understand the advantages, disadvantages, and good practices in personal use of e-mail, text/picture/video messaging, blogs, wikis, online social networks, Web conferences, and content sharing

Safe User, Protected from the Risks in a Digital World

Goal: I would like to take measures to (1) protect my computers, devices, and data from loss, damage, or misuse; (2) minimize or prevent risks associated with using technology; and (3) minimize the environmental impact of using computers and related devices.

Topic	Resource	Location	Now you should . . .
Viruses and Antivirus Programs	Text & FAQ	p. 110	Describe malware and its relationship to a computer virus
	FAQ Link and Video	eBook p. 110, or Computer Viruses link, CourseMate	
	Web Link	eBook p. 110 or CourseMate	
Mapping Services	Ethics & Issues	p. 129	Be aware of issues surrounding mapping services

Competent Digital Citizen

Goal: I would like to be knowledgeable and well-informed about computers, mobile devices, and related technology, so that I am digitally literate in my personal and professional use of digital devices.

Topic	Resource	Location	Now you should . . .
Application Software	Text/Figure	p. 108	Be able to identify the primary use of various application software
System Software	Text/Figure	pp. 108–109	Know the role of system software with respect to application software
	Figure 3-2 Animation	eBook p. 109 or CourseMate	

Continued on next page

Continued from previous page

Topic	Resource	Location	Now you should . . .
Fireworks Software	Innovative Computing	p. 120	Understand how fireworks shows use software to coordinate music with the display
	Link	eBook p. 120 or CourseMate	
Driving Aids	Looking Ahead	p. 127	Be familiar with developments underway to assist drivers
	Link and Video	eBook p. 127 or CourseMate	
Entertainment	Text/Figure and FAQ	p. 128	Know examples of entertainment software
	Web Link	eBook p. 128 or CourseMate	
	FAQ Link	eBook p.128, or Entertainment Software link, CourseMate	
Distance Learning	Text/Figure	p. 131	Be familiar with the uses and benefits of DL training and education
Dan Bricklin	Text	p. 133	Be familiar with Dan Bricklin's contributions to the software industry
	Link	eBook p. 133 or CourseMate	

Future Entrepreneur or Professional in a Digital Society

Goal: As I ponder my future, I envision myself as an entrepreneur or skilled professional using technology to support my business endeavors or job responsibilities. Along the way, I may interact with a variety of computer professionals — or I may just become one myself!

Topic	Resource	Location	Now you should . . .
Project Management	Text/Figure	p. 118	Know the purpose of project management software in business
Accounting Software	Text/Figure	p. 119	Know how companies use accounting software
Enterprise Computing	Text	p. 119	Know the functional business units that use specialized software
CAD	Text/Figure	p. 121	Know how engineers, architects, and scientists use CAD software
	Computer Usage @ Work	p. 132	
	Link and Video	eBook p. 132 or CourseMate	
DTP	Text/Figure	p. 121	Know how professional designers use DTP software
Paint/Image Editing	Text/Figure	p. 121	Know how professionals use paint/image editing software
Photo Editing	Text	p. 121	Know how photo editing software assists professional photo users
Video and Audio Editing	Text/Figure	p. 122	Know how professionals use video editing software and audio editing software
Multimedia Authoring	Text/Figure	p. 122	Know how multimedia authoring software is used in business
Web Page Authoring	Text/Figure	p. 122	Know the purpose of Web page authoring software
Help Desk Specialist	Exploring Computer Careers	CourseMate	Be familiar with the responsibilities of and education required for a help desk specialist
Digital Communications	Text/Figures	pp. 143, 145, 147, 149, 151, and 153	Understand the advantages, disadvantages, and good practices in business use of e-mail, text/picture/video/instant messaging, blogs, wikis, online social networks, Web conferences, and content sharing

Preparing for a Test

Visit the Computer Concepts CourseMate at www.cengagebrain.com and then navigate to the Chapter 3 Web Apps resource for this book to prepare for your test.

Does your class use the Computer Concepts CourseMate Web site? If so, prepare for your test by using the Flash Cards, Study Guide, and Practice Test Web apps — available for your smart phone or tablet.

If your class does not use the Computer Concepts CourseMate Web site or you prefer to use your book, you can prepare for the test by doing the Quiz Yourself activities on pages 112, 123, and 132; reading the Chapter Review on pages 134–135; ensuring you know the definitions for the terms on page 135; and completing the Checkpoint exercises on page 136. You also should know the material identified in the Chapter 3 Study Guide that follows.

Chapter 3 Study Guide

This study guide identifies material you should know for the Chapter 3 exam. You may want to write the answers in a notebook, enter them on your digital device, record them into a phone, or highlight them in your book. Choose whichever method helps you remember the best.

1. Identify four uses for application software.

2. Differentiate among packaged software, custom software, Web apps, open source software, shareware, freeware, and public-domain software.

3. Explain how the operating system and utility programs work with application software.

4. Name three popular personal computer operating systems.

5. Malicious software also is known as _____.

6. Identify ways a computer can be infected with a virus.

7. Describe common elements of the Windows user interface.

8. Explain the purpose of a file. Give an example of a file name.

9. Know how to start a Windows program.

10. Describe the features available in word processing software. Name popular word processing programs.

11. Explain the process of creating, editing, formatting, saving, and printing a document.

12. Font size is gauged by a measurement system called _____.

13. Describe the features of spreadsheet software and the organization of a spreadsheet. Name popular spreadsheet programs.

14. Define the term, database. Describe how a database is organized and the purpose of database software. Name popular database programs.

15. Describe the features available in presentation software. Name popular presentation programs.

16. Identify the function and benefit of note taking software.

17. Identify programs typically in a business software suite and advantages of using a suite. Name popular business software suites.

18. Identify types of business software available for phones.

19. Describe the purpose of project management software, accounting software, and document management software.

20. Adobe Reader enables you to view any _____ file.

21. Identify the functional business units in an enterprise that use specialized software.

22. Explain how engineers, architects, and scientists use CAD software.

23. Explain how professionals use DTP software, paint software, image editing software, photo editing software, video and editing software, and multimedia authoring software.

24. Identify the purpose and users of Web page authoring software.

25. Describe the benefits of personal finance software.

26. Identify the purpose of legal software.

27. Describe the purpose of tax preparation software.

28. Identify key features of these programs for personal use: desktop publishing, paint/image editing, photo editing, photo management, clip art/image gallery, video and audio editing, and home design/landscaping.

29. Describe features of travel and mapping software.

30. Describe types of reference software and educational software.

31. Identify some uses of computer-based training.

32. Describe types of entertainment software.

33. Describe the purpose of a Web app and various distribution methods. Name popular Web apps.

34. Identify issues surrounding online mapping services.

35. Describe the purpose of these application programs for communications: Web browser, e-mail, text/picture/video messaging, RSS aggregator, blogging, FTP, VoIP, and video conferencing.

Continued on next page

Continued from previous page

---

36. Define the terms, online Help and Web-based Help.

37. Define the term, Web-based training.

38. Explain the purpose of distance learning and e-learning.

39. Identify the names of Adobe's widely used programs.

40. Identify some of Microsoft's products and services.

41. Identify the advantages of personal and business use with e-mail, text/picture/video messaging, blogs, wikis, online social networks, Web conferences, and content sharing.

Check This Out

As technology changes, you must keep up with updates, new products, breakthroughs, and recent advances to remain digitally literate. The list below identifies topics related to this chapter that you should explore to keep current. In parentheses beside each topic, you will find a search term to help begin your research using a search engine, such as Google.

For current news and information
Check us out on Facebook and Twitter. See your instructor or the Computer Concepts CourseMate for specific information.

1. **widely used freeware** (search for: popular freeware)

2. **malware attacks on mobile devices** (search for: mobile malware)

3. **business letter writing tips** (search for: writing business letters)

4. **presentation software design principles** (search for: presentation software slide design)

5. **business software apps for smart phones** (search for: best business apps)

6. **latest version of Adobe Reader** (search for: Adobe Reader version)

7. **check deposit using a smart phone** (search for: remote deposit smart phone)

8. **popular photo editing software** (search for: best photo editing software)

9. **widely used computer games** (search for: top computer games)

10. **current productivity Web apps** (search for: productivity Web apps)

11. **new iTunes U course lectures** (search for: iTunes U lectures)

12. **recent computer viruses** (search for: latest computer viruses)

13. **latest Microsoft news** (search for: Microsoft news)

14. **latest news about online social networks** (search for: social network news)

15. **top blogs** (search for: best blogs)

Chapter 4

The Components of the System Unit

Why Should I Learn About System Unit Components?

"I bought my computer a few years ago, and it appears to be working well. Although at times it seems to run a little slow and it generates a lot of heat, I have not had problems with it. So, why do I need to learn about hardware in the system unit?"

True, you may be familiar with some of the material in this chapter, but do you know . . .

"Why do I need to learn about hardware in the system unit?"

- How computer chips can help you locate a lost pet? (p. 158, Innovative Computing)
- How manufacturers name their processors? (p. 161, Comparison of Personal Computer Processors)
- Why the Department of Homeland Security may search your notebook computer at the airport? (p. 176, Ethics & Issues)
- How the sports industry uses computers? (p. 178, Computer Usage @ Work)
- Which company is the world's leading chip manufacturer? (p. 179, Companies on the Cutting Edge)
- How to purchase and install computer memory? (pp. 184–185 and Computer Concepts CourseMate, Learn How To)
- How to monitor your computer's electric consumption? (Windows Exercises, Computer Concepts CourseMate)

For these answers and to discover much more information essential to this course, read Chapter 4 and visit the associated Computer Concepts CourseMate at www.cengagebrain.com.

Customize Your Learning Experience

Q&A How can I meet one or more of these goals?

Make use of the goal's resources for each chapter in the book and you should meet that goal by the end of the course.

Adapt this book to meet your needs by determining your goal. Would you like to be an informed digital consumer? A productive technology user? A safe user, protected from the risks in a digital world? A competent digital citizen? A future entrepreneur or professional in a digital society?

Every chapter in this Student Success Guide identifies resources targeted toward each of these goals, along with criteria to verify you understand the resources' content. Resources may be located in the textbook, on the Computer Concepts CourseMate Web site, in the interactive eBook, and on the Web.

Informed Digital Consumer

Goal: I would like to understand the terminology used in Web or print advertisements that sell computers, mobile devices, and related technology, as well as the jargon used by sales associates in computer or electronics stores, so that I can make informed purchasing decisions.

Topic	Resource	Location	Now you should . . .
ID Chips	Innovative Computing	p. 158	Know how ID chips help locate lost pets, along with other uses of the chips and approximate cost
	Link	eBook p. 158 or CourseMate	
Personal Computer Processors	Text	p. 161	Be familiar with processor chip manufacturers
Memory Sizes	Text/Figure	p. 164	Know the terms and acronyms used to define memory sizes
	Drag and Drop Figure 4-11	eBook p. 164 or CourseMate	

Continued on next page

Continued from previous page

Topic	Resource	Location	Now you should . . .
RAM Types and Requirements	Text/Figures	pp. 164–166	Know the types of RAM chips and guidelines for amount of RAM needed when purchasing or upgrading
	FAQ and Link	eBook p. 166 or CourseMate	
	Learn How To	pp. 184–185	
Cache	Text	p. 167	Know the types of cache and their capacities
Memory Access Times	Text/Figures	p. 168	Know the terms and acronyms used to define memory access times
	Drag and Drop Figure 4-15	eBook p. 168 or CourseMate	
Adapter Cards	Text/Figure	p. 169	Know the purpose of widely used types of adapter cards
	Drag and Drop Figure 4-17	eBook p. 169 or CourseMate	
Video Cards, etc.	Web Link	eBook p. 169 or CourseMate	Be familiar with video cards and other components you can purchase
Removable Flash Memory	Text/Figure	pp. 169–170	Be familiar with the purpose and use of memory cards, USB flash drives, and ExpressCard modules
Ports and Connectors	Text/Figures	pp. 170–171	Know the purpose of and be able to identify ports on desktop computers, notebook computers, and mobile devices
Processor and RAM	Figure 4-26	p. 176	Be familiar with processor and RAM recommendations for various users
NVIDIA	Text	p. 179	Be familiar with NVIDIA's products
	Link	eBook p. 179 or CourseMate	
Intel	Text	p. 179	Be familiar with Intel's products
	Link and Video	eBook p. 179 or CourseMate	

Productive Technology User

Goal: I would like to learn ways that technology can benefit me at home, work, and school. I also would like to learn helpful techniques for using technology so that I can perform tasks more efficiently and be more productive in daily activities.

Topic	Resource	Location	Now you should . . .
System Clock	Windows Exercises	CourseMate	Be able to set the system clock on a Windows computer
Flash Memory	Text/Figure	p. 167	Know examples of flash memory and how mobile devices use it
Portable Media Players	Figure and FAQ	p. 167	Know how portable media players store music
	FAQ Link	eBook p. 167, or Portable Media Players link, CourseMate	
USB Ports	Text/Figure	p. 171	Know how to use a USB port
	Web Link	eBook p. 171 or CourseMate	
FireWire	Text	p. 172	Know how FireWire works
	Web Link	eBook p. 172 or CourseMate	
Installing Hardware	Windows Exercises	CourseMate	Be able to install a new device

Continued on next page

Continued from previous page

Topic	Resource	Location	Now you should . . .
Port Replicators and Docking Stations	Text/Figure	p. 173	Know the purpose of port replicators and docking stations
Bays	Text/Figure	p. 175	Know and be able to identify various types of bays
Power Supply and Fans	Text and FAQ	p. 175	Be familiar with the role of the power supply
Apps for Sports Fans	Computer Usage @ Work Video	eBook p. 178 or CourseMate	Be familiar with phone and tablet apps for professional baseball and football
Installing RAM	Learn How To	pp. 184–185	Know how to install RAM
Time Machine	Video	At the Movies, CourseMate	Know how to use Time Machine on an Apple computer to restore any previous files, data, or programs
Calculator	Labs	CourseMate	Know how to use Windows Calculator
	Windows Exercises		
Google Docs	Web Apps	CourseMate	Know how to use Google Docs to create documents, presentations, and spreadsheets

Safe User, Protected from the Risks in a Digital World

Goal: I would like to take measures to (1) protect my computers, devices, and data from loss, damage, or misuse; (2) minimize or prevent risks associated with using technology; and (3) minimize the environmental impact of using computers and related devices.

Topic	Resource	Location	Now you should . . .
Computer Search and Seizure	Ethics & Issues	p. 176	Be aware that the Dept. of Homeland Security can search and seize any mobile computer or device upon its arrival in the U.S.
Cleaning Computers and Mobile Devices	Text/Figure and FAQ	p. 177	Know how to keep your computer and mobile device clean
Power Management	Windows Exercises	CourseMate	Be able to manage the power usage on your computer

Competent Digital Citizen

Goal: I would like to be knowledgeable and well-informed about computers, mobile devices, and related technology, so that I am digitally literate in my personal and professional use of digital devices.

Topic	Resource	Location	Now you should . . .
System Units	Text/Figures	pp. 156–157	Know size and shape of system units on various computers and devices
Motherboard	Text/Figure	p. 158	Recognize the various slots, chips, and other items on a motherboard
	Labs	CourseMate	

Continued on next page

Continued from previous page

Topic	Resource	Location	Now you should . . .
System Unit Components	Drag and Drop Figure 4-3	p. 158	Be able to identify the items in and on a system unit
Processor	Text/Figures	p. 159–160	Know the purpose of processors, relative speed of multi-core processors, and the role of the control unit and ALU
	Drag and Drop Figure 4-4	p. 159	
	Web Link	eBook p. 159 or CourseMate	
Machine Cycle	Text/Figures	p. 160	Know the steps in a machine cycle and their relationship to processing speed
	Figure 4-5 Animation	p. 160	
System Clock	Text	pp. 160–161	Know the purpose of the system clock and how clock speed is measured
Data Representation	Text/Figures	pp. 162–163	Understand how a computer represents data
	Labs	CourseMate	
Memory Storage	Text/Figure	p. 164	Know what items memory stores and how items are stored
Memory Types	Text	p. 164	Understand the difference between volatile and nonvolatile memory and types of RAM
RAM	Text/Figure	pp. 164–165	Understand how program instructions transfer in and out of RAM
	Labs	CourseMate	Know the technical details about how RAM works
One Laptop per Child	Ethics & Issues	p. 166	Know the intent of the OLPC plan endorsed by the United Nations
	Video		See how the OLPCs work
ROM	Text	p. 167	Understand the purpose of ROM chips
	Labs	CourseMate	
CMOS	Text	p. 168	Be able to identify examples of CMOS use
Future Notebook Computers	Looking Ahead	p. 173	Know some of the current and future developments with respect to notebook computers
	Link and Video	eBook p. 173 or CourseMate	
Buses	Text/Figure	p. 174	Know the parts of a bus, bus widths, and types of buses
Computers in Sports	Computer Usage @ Work	p. 178	Recognize how computers are used in professional baseball and NASCAR
	Link		
Jack Kilby	Text	p. 179	Be familiar with Jack Kilby's most significant patent
	Link	eBook p. 179 or CourseMate	
Gordon Moore	Text	p. 179	Be familiar with Moore's Law and other contributions from Gordon Moore
	Link	eBook p. 179 or CourseMate	

Future Entrepreneur or Professional in a Digital Society

Goal: As I ponder my future, I envision myself as an entrepreneur or skilled professional using technology to support my business endeavors or job responsibilities. Along the way, I may interact with a variety of computer professionals — or I may just become one myself!

Topic	Resource	Location	Now you should . . .
PC Market Share	FAQ	p. 161	Know the top PC vendors
Computer Factory	FAQ Video	eBook p. 161 or CourseMate	See how one PC vendor manufactures computers and fulfills orders
Computer Engineer	Exploring Computer Careers	CourseMate	Be familiar with the responsibilities of and education required for a computer engineer

Preparing for a Test

Visit the Computer Concepts CourseMate at www.cengagebrain.com and then navigate to the Chapter 4 Web Apps resource for this book to prepare for your test.

Does your class use the Computer Concepts CourseMate Web site? If so, prepare for your test by using the Flash Cards, Study Guide, and Practice Test Web apps — available for your smart phone or tablet.

If your class does not use the Computer Concepts CourseMate Web site or you prefer to use your book, you can prepare for the test by doing the Quiz Yourself activities on pages 161, 168, and 178; reading the Chapter Review on pages 180–181; ensuring you know the definitions for the terms on page 181; and completing the Checkpoint exercises on page 182. You also should know the material identified in the Chapter 4 Study Guide that follows.

Chapter 4 Study Guide

This study guide identifies material you should know for the Chapter 4 exam. You may want to write the answers in a notebook, enter them on your digital device, record them into a phone, or highlight them in your book. Choose whichever method helps you remember the best.

1. Differentiate among the various styles of system units on desktop computers, notebook computers, and mobile devices.
2. Define the term, motherboard. Identify components that attach to the motherboard.
3. Define the term, computer chip.
4. Describe uses of chip implants.
5. A processor also is called a CPU, which stands for _____.
6. Describe the purpose of a processor. Describe multi-core processors.
7. Explain the role of the control unit and ALU in a computer.
8. Explain the four steps in a machine cycle.
9. Identify the purpose of the system clock. Explain its relationship to the processor and devices.
10. One _____ (GHz) equals one billion ticks of the system clock per second.
11. The leading manufacturers of personal computer processor chips are _____ and _____.
12. Explain how processor manufacturers identify their chips.
13. Define the term, bit. The two digits used to represent bits are the _____ and _____.
14. Describe how a series of bits represents data.
15. Define the term, memory. Describe three types of items it stores.
16. Explain how memory uses addresses.
17. Differentiate among a kilobyte, megabyte, gigabyte, and terabyte. State their abbreviations.
18. Explain the difference between volatile and nonvolatile memory.
19. Explain how program instructions transfer in and out of memory.
20. Differentiate among DRAM, SRAM, and MRAM.
21. RAM chips usually reside on a _____ module.
22. Describe how to determine the amount of RAM necessary in a computer.
23. State the purpose of memory cache. Describe three types of memory cache.
24. Define the terms, ROM and firmware.
25. Define flash memory. Identify examples of its use.
26. Describe the advantage and uses of CMOS technology.
27. Define access time.

Continued on next page

Continued from previous page

28. Differentiate among a millisecond, microsecond, nanosecond, and picosecond. State their abbreviations.

29. Describe the purpose of expansion slots and adapter cards.

30. Differentiate among a sound card, network card, and video card.

31. Differentiate among a memory card, USB flash drive, PC Card, and ExpressCard module.

32. Explain the difference between a port and a connector.

33. Differentiate between a USB port and a FireWire port.

34. Explain the purpose of USB and FireWire hubs.

35. Briefly describe the purpose of a Bluetooth port, SCSI port, eSATA port, IrDA port, serial port, and MIDI port.

36. Explain the purpose of a port replicator and docking station.

37. Define the terms, bus and bus width.

38. Describe the purpose of a front side bus, backside bus, and expansion buses.

39. Explain the purpose of a power supply.

40. Describe Moore's Law.

Check This Out

As technology changes, you must keep up with updates, new products, breakthroughs, and recent advances to remain digitally literate. The list below identifies topics related to this chapter that you should explore to keep current. In parentheses beside each topic, you will find a search term to help begin your research using a search engine, such as Google.

For current news and information
Check us out on Facebook and Twitter. See your instructor or the Computer Concepts CourseMate for specific information.

1. **latest tablet computers** (search for: tablets)

2. **recent uses of robotic technologies** (search for: new robot trends)

3. **fastest processor clock speeds** (search for: fastest processor)

4. **latest personal computer processors** (search for: processor comparison)

5. **top personal computer vendors** (search for: personal computer market share)

6. **new liquid cooling technology** (search for: liquid cooled computers)

7. **recent computer memory developments** (search for: new computer memory)

8. **One Laptop per Child notebook computers** (search for: OLPC stories)

9. **new removable flash memory devices** (search for: flash memory update)

10. **latest USB developments** (search for: USB news)

11. **latest Bluetooth technologies** (search for: Bluetooth improvements)

12. **docking stations for mobile devices** (search for: mobile device docking station)

13. **power supply heat problems** (search for: computer power supply heat)

14. **tablet computer use in professional sports** (search for: tablet professional sports)

15. **predictions based on Moore's Law** (search for: Moore's Law future)

Input and Output

Why Should I Learn About Input Devices?

"After work or school, I video chat with my friends and discuss our gaming strategies. We watch sports on my HDTV and print fantasy team rosters on my ink-jet printer. My wireless surround sound system makes us feel like we have front-row stadium seats. What other input and output devices could I possibly use?"

True, you may be familiar with some of the material in this chapter, but do you know . . .

"What other input and output devices could I possibly use?"

- How to reduce the risk of injuring your wrists when you are typing? (p. 191, Keyboard Ergonomics)
- Which tabletop display Microsoft developed that has a touch screen and the ability to recognize fingers and objects? (p. 193, Touch Screens and Touch-Sensitive Pads)
- Which features to consider when purchasing an LCD screen or monitor? (pp. 208–209, LCD Quality)
- Where you can discard depleted toner cartridges in an environmentally safe manner? (p. 215, FAQ)
- Who conceptualized the computer mouse more than 60 years ago? (p. 223, Technology Trailblazers)
- How to make a video and upload it to YouTube? (pp. 228–229 and Computer Concepts CourseMate, Learn How To)
- How to use video editing software? (p. 348, Digital Video Technology Special Feature)
- Which Windows options assist those with hearing or visual impairments? (Windows Exercises, Computer Concepts CourseMate)

For these answers and to discover much more information essential to this course, read Chapter 5 and visit the associated Computer Concepts CourseMate at www.cengagebrain.com.

Customize Your Learning Experience

Q&A How can I meet one or more of these goals?

Make use of the goal's resources for each chapter in the book and you should meet that goal by the end of the course.

Adapt this book to meet your needs by determining your goal. Would you like to be an informed digital consumer? A productive technology user? A safe user, protected from the risks in a digital world? A competent digital citizen? A future entrepreneur or professional in a digital society?

Every chapter in this Student Success Guide identifies resources targeted toward each of these goals, along with criteria to verify you understand the resources' content. Resources may be located in the textbook, on the Computer Concepts CourseMate Web site, in the interactive eBook, and on the Web.

Informed Digital Consumer

Goal: I would like to understand the terminology used in Web or print advertisements that sell computers, mobile devices, and related technology, as well as the jargon used by sales associates in computer or electronics stores, so that I can make informed purchasing decisions.

Topic	Resource	Location	Now you should . . .
Mouse Types	Text/Figures	pp. 191–192	Know the mouse types including optical, laser, air, and wireless
Portable Media Player	FAQ	p. 194	Know which companies sell the most portable media players
Smart Phone	Text/Figure	pp. 195–196	Be familiar with various types of input for smart phones

Continued on next page

Continued from previous page

Topic	Resource	Location	Now you should . . .
Game Controllers	Text/Figures	pp. 196–197	Be able to identify and know the purpose of various game controllers
	Drag and Drop Figure 5-13	eBook p. 196 or CourseMate	
	Web Link		Know about the Wii Remote
	Video		Know about the xBox Kinect
Digital Camera Types	Text	p. 197	Know the differences of studio, field, and point-and-shoot cameras
Resolution	Text/Figure	p. 198	Be able to explain resolution and its relationship to digital cameras
Web Cams	Text/Figure	p. 199	Know the purpose and approximate costs of Web cams
Bar Code Reader	Video	eBook p. 201 or CourseMate	Be familiar with the benefits of a bar code reader
Terminals	Text/Figures	pp. 204–205	Know the purpose and uses of POS terminals, ATMs, and DVD kiosks
LCD Monitors and Screens	Text/Figures	p. 208	Be familiar with features of LCD monitors and screens
	Web Link	eBook p. 208 or CourseMate	
	Video	At the Movies, CourseMate	
Digital Frames	Innovative Computing	p. 209	Be familiar with the features and costs of digital frames
	Link and Video	eBook p. 209 or CourseMate	
LCD Quality	Text/Figures	p. 209	Know the factors that affect quality of an LCD monitor or screen
Plasma Monitors	Text/Figure	p. 210	Be familiar with the features of plasma monitors
Printer Purchase	Text/Figure	p. 211	Be familiar with questions to ask when purchasing a printer
Ink-Jet Printers	Text/Figures	pp. 213–214	Know the features, resolution, and costs of ink-jet printers and ink
Photo Printers	Text/Figure	p. 214	Know the features and uses of photo printers
	Web Link	eBook p. 214 or CourseMate	
Laser Printers	Text/Figure	pp. 214–215	Know the features and costs of laser printers and toner
	Web Link	eBook p. 215 or CourseMate	
Multifunction Peripherals	Text/Figure	p. 215	Know the features, advantages, and disadvantages of multifunction peripherals
Speakers	Text/Figure	p. 217	Be familiar with the features of speakers
Headphones and Earbuds	Text/Figures	pp. 217–218	Know the difference between headphones, earbuds, and headsets
	Web Link	eBook p. 218 or CourseMate	
Recommended Device	Text/Figure	p. 219	Be familiar with input and output device recommendations
Logitech	Text	p. 223	Be familiar with Logitech's recent products
	Link	eBook p. 223 or CourseMate	
HP	Text	p. 223	Be familiar with HP's products and services
	Link	eBook p. 223 or CourseMate	
Digital Video Technology	Text/Figures	pp. 231–236	Know how to select a video camera, record a video, transfer and manage videos, edit videos, and distribute videos
	Figure 5-3 Animation	p. 232	

Productive Technology User

Goal: I would like to learn ways that technology can benefit me at home, work, and school. I also would like to learn helpful techniques for using technology so that I can perform tasks more efficiently and be more productive in daily activities.

Topic	Resource	Location	Now you should . . .
Keyboard Keys	Text/Figure	p. 190	Be able to identify and know the function of various keyboard keys
	Drag and Drop Figure 5-2	CourseMate	
Mobile Computer and Device Keyboards	Text/Figure	p. 191	Know the types of keyboards on notebook computers and mobile devices
	Drag and Drop Figure 5-3	eBook p. 191 or CourseMate	
Other Pointing Devices	Text/Figures	p. 192	Know the look and purpose of a trackball, touchpad, and pointing stick
Touch Screens	Text/Figures	p. 193	Know the function of touch screens and their various uses
	Web Link	eBook p. 193 or CourseMate	Be familiar with various multi-touch screen uses
Touch-Sensitive Pads	Text/Figure	p. 193	Know the functions of a touch-sensitive pad and its uses
Stylus and Digital Pen	Text/Figure	p. 194	Be familiar with the purpose of a stylus and digital pen
Digital Camera Use	Text/Figure	pp. 197–198	Know the ways users work with images from a digital camera and how a digital camera works
	Figure 5-14 Animation	eBook p. 197 or CourseMate	
Voice and Audio Input	Text/Figure	p. 198	Know the uses of voice and audio input
	Labs	CourseMate	Know how to import and download audio files, and burn audio CDs
DV Cameras	Text	p. 199	Know how users work with digital video cameras
Video Editing	Video	At the Movies, CourseMate	Know how to edit videos, import clips, and work with clips and transitions
	Labs	CourseMate	
Flatbed Scanner	Text/Figures	p. 200	Know how flatbed scanners work and the benefit of OCR software
Monitors	Text	p. 207	Know adjustments available on computer monitors
Graphics Ports	Text	p. 209	Be familiar with the purpose of DVI and HDMI
	Web Link	eBook p. 209 or CourseMate	
Printing Methods	Text/Figure	p. 212	Be familiar with the various printing methods
Accessibility Options, Paint, and Sound	Windows Exercises	CourseMate	Know how to use Sound Sentry, Narrator, and Magnifier in Windows; how to use Paint; and how to adjust sound
Make and Upload a Video	Learn How To	pp. 228–229 and CourseMate	Know how to transfer a video to a computer, upload the video to YouTube, and view the video
Sending Files	Web Apps	CourseMate	Know how to use YouSendIt

Safe User, Protected from the Risks in a Digital World

Goal: I would like to take measures to (1) protect my computers, devices, and data from loss, damage, or misuse; (2) minimize or prevent risks associated with using technology; and (3) minimize the environmental impact of using computers and related devices.

Topic	Resource	Location	Now you should . . .
Ergonomics	Text	p. 190	Know the purpose of ergonomics and the latest information about it
	Web Link	eBook p. 190 or CourseMate	

Continued on next page

Continued from previous page

Topic	Resource	Location	Now you should . . .
RSIs	FAQ	p. 191	Know ways to reduce your chance of experiencing RSIs and recognize symptoms
	Link and Video	eBook p. 191 or CourseMate	
	Ethics & Issues	p. 192	Know the issues surrounding workplace RSIs
Biometric Monitoring	Ethics & Issues	p. 203	Be aware of privacy issues surrounding biometric facial recognition
	Video	eBook p. 203 or CourseMate	
Toner Disposal	FAQ	p. 215	Know how to dispose of toner cartridges properly
	Link and Video	eBook p. 215 or CourseMate	Be familiar with recycling guidelines

Competent Digital Citizen

Goal: I would like to be knowledgeable and well-informed about computers, mobile devices, and related technology, so that I am digitally literate in my personal and professional use of digital devices.

Topic	Resource	Location	Now you should . . .
Input	Text/Figure	pp. 188–189	Be able to identify various input devices
Optical Readers	Text/Figures	p. 200	Know the difference between OCR and OMR
Bar Code Readers	Text/Figure	p. 201	Know the purpose of bar code readers and uses of bar codes
RFID Readers	Text/Figure	p. 201	Know the purpose of RFID readers and uses of RFID tags
Magstripe Reader	Text/Figure	p. 201	Be familiar with magstripe readers and what is stored in stripes
MICR	Text/Figure	p. 202	Know the purpose of MICR readers and what they read on a check
Biometric Input	Text/Figure	pp. 202–203	Know the purpose and uses of various biometric devices
	Link	eBook p. 203 or CourseMate	
Output	Text/Figures	pp. 206–207	Be able to identify various output devices
Display Devices	Text/Figures	pp. 207–208	Be familiar with display devices on various computers and devices
	Labs	CourseMate	
Video Content	FAQ	p. 210	Know the type of video content most often viewed
	FAQ Link	eBook p. 211, or Video Output Content link, CourseMate	Know about video apps
CRT Monitors	Text/Figure	pp. 210–211	Know how CRT monitors work
Nonimpact Printers	Text	p. 213	Describe how nonimpact printers work and name examples
	Labs	CourseMate	
Input and Output Devices for Physically Challenged Users	Text/Figures	pp. 220–221	Be familiar with input and output devices designed to assist users who are physically challenged
	Ethics & Issues		
	Looking Ahead		
	Video and Link	eBook p. 221 or CourseMate	
Computers in Space Exploration	Computer Usage @ Work	p. 222	Recognize how computers are used in space exploration
	Link and Video	eBook p. 222 or CourseMate	
Douglas Engelbart	Text	p. 223	Be familiar with Douglas Engelbart's contribution to the computing industry
	Link	eBook p. 223 or CourseMate	
Ursula Burns	Text	p. 223	Know the company of which Ursula Burns is chair and CEO
	Link	eBook p. 223 or CourseMate	

Future Entrepreneur or Professional in a Digital Society

Goal: As I ponder my future, I envision myself as an entrepreneur or skilled professional using technology to support my business endeavors or job responsibilities. Along the way, I may interact with a variety of computer professionals — or I may just become one myself!

Topic	Resource	Location	Now you should . . .
Graphics Tablet	Text/Figure	p. 194	Know how professionals use a graphics tablet
Web Cams	Text	p. 199	Know how businesses might use a Web cam
Video Conference	Text/Figure	p. 199	Know how a video conference works
RFID Readers	Text/Figure	p. 201	Know why some retailers prefer RFID to bar code technology
Thermal Printers	Text/Figure	p. 215	Know the uses of thermal printers in businesses
Mobile Printers	Text/Figure	p. 216	Know the features of mobile printers
Plotters and Large-Format Printers	Text/Figure	p. 216	Know the features and uses of plotters and large-format printers
	Figure Video	eBook p. 216 or CourseMate	
Data Projectors	Text/Figure	p. 218	Know the function of data projectors
Interactive Whiteboards	Text/Figure	p. 218	Know the function, technologies, and uses of interactive whiteboards
	Link and Video	eBook p. 218 or CourseMate	
3-D Graphics	Labs	CourseMate	Know how 3-D graphics work
Graphic Designer/ Illustrator	Exploring Computer Careers	CourseMate	Be familiar with the responsibilities of and education required for a graphic designer/illustrator

Preparing for a Test

Visit the Computer Concepts CourseMate at www.cengagebrain.com and then navigate to the Chapter 5 Web Apps resource for this book to prepare for your test.

Does your class use the Computer Concepts CourseMate Web site? If so, prepare for your test by using the Flash Cards, Study Guide, and Practice Test Web apps — available for your smart phone or tablet.

If your class does not use the Computer Concepts CourseMate Web site or you prefer to use your book, you can prepare for the test by doing the Quiz Yourself activities on pages 195, 205, 211, and 222; reading the Chapter Review on pages 224–225; ensuring you know the definitions for the terms on page 225; and completing the Checkpoint exercises on pages 226–227. You also should know the material identified in the Chapter 5 Study Guide that follows.

Chapter 5 Study Guide

This study guide identifies material you should know for the Chapter 5 exam. You may want to write the answers in a notebook, enter them on your digital device, record them into a phone, or highlight them in your book. Choose whichever method helps you remember the best.

1. Define the terms, input and input device.
2. Identify the function of commonly used keys and buttons on desktop computer keyboards.
3. Identify two types of wireless technologies that a wireless keyboard or wireless mouse might use.
4. The goal of _____ is to incorporate comfort, efficiency, and safety in the design of the workplace.
5. Identify ways to reduce chances of experiencing RSIs.
6. Describe the differences among mouse types: optical mouse, laser mouse, air mouse, and wireless mouse.
7. Describe a trackball, touchpad, and pointing stick.
8. Identify uses of touch screens.
9. Explain how to use a touch-sensitive pad.
10. Describe various types of pen input.
11. Identify various types of input for smart phones.
12. Summarize the purpose of various game controllers: gamepads, joysticks and wheels, light guns, dance pads, and motion-sensing game controllers.
13. Differentiate among types of digital cameras: studio, field, and point-and-shoot.

Continued on next page

Continued from previous page

14. Explain how resolution affects the quality of a picture captured on a digital camera.

15. MP stands for _____.

16. Describe the uses of voice input.

17. Describe a DV camera.

18. Identify the purpose of a Web cam.

19. Describe how a video conference works.

20. Describe the purpose of a flatbed scanner. Identify the purpose of OCR software.

21. Describe how optical readers work. Differentiate between OCR and OMR. Give examples of their uses.

22. Describe bar code readers. Identify uses of bar codes.

23. Describe how RFID readers work. State uses of RFID tags.

24. Identify the purpose of magstripe readers. State types of information stored on a stripe.

25. The _____ industry almost exclusively uses MICR readers.

26. Define the term, biometrics.

27. Describe the purpose and use of these biometric devices: fingerprint reader, face recognition system, hand geometry system, voice verification system, signature verification system, and iris recognition system.

28. Identify the purpose of POS terminals, ATMs, and DVD kiosks.

29. PIN stands for _____.

30. Define the terms, output and output device.

31. Identify ways most monitors can be adjusted.

32. Identify characteristics of LCD monitors and LCD screens.

33. LCD stands for _____.

34. Describe the factors that affect the quality of an LCD monitor or LCD screen: resolution, response time, brightness, dot pitch, and contrast ratio.

35. Differentiate between DVI and HDMI ports.

36. Explain the characteristics of plasma monitors.

37. Identify questions to ask when purchasing a printer.

38. Describe various ways to print.

39. Differentiate between a nonimpact and an impact printer.

40. Describe characteristics and uses of ink-jet printers, photo printers, laser printers, multifunction peripherals, thermal printers, mobile printers, and plotters and large-format printers.

41. Identify proper ways to dispose of toner cartridges.

42. Describe the uses of speakers. Differentiate among headphones, headsets, and earbuds.

43. Identify the purpose of data projectors and interactive whiteboards.

44. Briefly describe the Americans with Disabilities Act. Identify input and output options for physically challenged users.

45. Identify types of devices sold by Logitech.

46. Identify products manufactured by HP.

47. Describe how to transfer videos from a DV camera to a computer. Explain ways to edit a video.

Check This Out

As technology changes, you must keep up with updates, new products, breakthroughs, and recent advances to remain digitally literate. The list below identifies topics related to this chapter that you should explore to keep current. In parentheses beside each topic, you will find a search term to help begin your research using a search engine, such as Google.

For current news and information
Check us out on Facebook and Twitter. See your instructor or the Computer Concepts CourseMate for specific information.

1. **new pointing devices** (search for: latest pointing devices)

2. **input devices for smart phones** (search for: new smart phone input devices)

3. **popular game controllers** (search for: game controllers)

4. **widely used digital camera features** (search for: digital camera specification review)

5. **new 3-D digital video cameras features** (search for: 3D video camera)

6. **video conferences using mobile devices** (search for: mobile device video conferencing)

7. **new biometric input devices** (search for: biometric devices)

8. **top LCD monitors** (search for: LCD monitor reviews)

9. **best ink-jet printers** (search for: top ink jet printers)

10. **latest photo printer characteristics** (search for: photo printer features)

11. **new laser printers** (search for: latest laser printers)

12. **widely used multifunction products** (search for: multifunction peripherals)

13. **latest wireless speaker systems** (search for: wireless speakers)

14. **new devices for physically challenged users** (search for: devices physically challenged)

15. **latest digital video technology** (search for: digital video equipment)

Why Should I Learn About Storage?

"My USB flash drive stores all the files I need for my classes. I transfer all of my digital photos from an SD card to my computer's hard disk, which also has plenty of space for my programs and music. Weekly, I back up files on my computer to an external hard disk. What other types of storage could I need?"

True, you may be familiar with some of the material in this chapter, but do you know . . .

"What other types of storage could I need?"

- How your hard disk reads and writes data? (p. 243, How a Hard Disk Works)
- How to safeguard data on your mobile media when traveling on commercial aircraft? (p. 250, FAQ)
- Where you can save and share your audio, video, graphics, and other important files on the Internet? (p. 251, Cloud Storage)
- When law enforcement officials may read your e-mail messages? (p. 252, Ethics & Issues)
- How meteorologists use computers to forecast storms and hurricanes? (p. 260, Computer Usage @ Work)
- Which company developed the first hard disk for the personal computer? (p. 261, Companies on the Cutting Edge)
- How to increase space on your hard disk? (p. 266 and Computer Concepts CourseMate, Learn How To)
- How to recover a file you deleted accidentally? (Windows Exercises, Computer Concepts CourseMate)

For these answers and to discover much more information essential to this course, read Chapter 6 and visit the associated Computer Concepts CourseMate at www.cengagebrain.com.

Customize Your Learning Experience

Q & A How can I meet one or more of these goals?

Make use of the goal's resources for each chapter in the book and you should meet that goal by the end of the course.

Adapt this book to meet your needs by determining your goal. Would you like to be an informed digital consumer? A productive technology user? A safe user, protected from the risks in a digital world? A competent digital citizen? A future entrepreneur or professional in a digital society?

Every chapter in this Student Success Guide identifies resources targeted toward each of these goals, along with criteria to verify you understand the resources' content. Resources may be located in the textbook, on the Computer Concepts CourseMate Web site, in the interactive eBook, and on the Web.

Informed Digital Consumer

Goal: I would like to understand the terminology used in Web or print advertisements that sell computers, mobile devices, and related technology, as well as the jargon used by sales associates in computer or electronics stores, so that I can make informed purchasing decisions.

Topic	Resource	Location	Now you should . . .
Storage Capacity	Text/Figure	p. 240	Know the terms and abbreviations that define capacity of storage media
	Drag and Drop Figure 6-2	eBook p. 240 or CourseMate	
Hard Disks	Text	pp. 240–244	Know the purpose of hard disks, their capacities, and uses
RAID	Text	p. 244	Know the purpose of RAID

Continued on next page

Continued from previous page

Topic	Resource	Location	Now you should . . .
External Hard Disks	Text/Figures	pp. 244–245	Know the capacities and advantages of external and removable hard disks
Hard Disk Controllers	Text	p. 246	Know the differences of SATA, EIDE, SCSI, and SAS controllers
	Web Link	eBook p. 246 or CourseMate	
SSDs	Text/Figure	p. 247	Know the purpose, form factors, capacities, advantages, and disadvantages of solid state drives
	Web Link	eBook p. 247 or CourseMate	
Memory Cards	Text/Figures	pp. 248–249	Know the types, capacities, and uses of various memory cards
	Web Link	eBook p. 249 or CourseMate	
USB Flash Drives	Text/Figure	p. 250	Know the uses and capacities of USB flash drives
ExpressCard Modules	Text/Figure	p. 250	Know the uses and sizes of ExpressCard modules
Optical Discs	Text/Figure	p. 252	Know the uses and sizes of optical discs
Optical Disc Types	Text/Figure	p. 253	Know the various optical disc formats and their capabilities
	Drag and Drop Figure 6-21	eBook p. 253 or CourseMate	
CDs	Text/Figure	pp. 254–255	Know the purpose and capacities of CD media and their drive speeds
Archive Disc	Text/Figure	p. 255	Know the use and cost of an archive disc or Picture CD
DVDs	Text/Figures	pp. 256–257	Know the use and storage capacities of various DVD media
Blu-Ray	Text/Figure	p. 256	Know the use and storage capacities of Blu-ray media
	Web Link	eBook p. 256 or CourseMate	
Seagate	Text	p. 261	Be familiar with Seagate's products
	Link and Video	eBook p. 261 or CourseMate	
SanDisk	Text	p. 261	Be familiar with SanDisk's products
	Link	eBook p. 261 or CourseMate	

Productive Technology User

Goal: I would like to learn ways that technology can benefit me at home, work, and school. I also would like to learn helpful techniques for using technology so that I can perform tasks more efficiently and be more productive in daily activities.

Topic	Resource	Location	Now you should . . .
Miniature Hard Disks	Text/Figures	p. 245	Know the uses of miniature hard disks
Cloud Storage	Text/Figures	pp. 251–252	Know the purpose, advantages, services offered, and providers of cloud storage
	Innovative Computing	p. 251	
	Link and Video	eBook p. 251 or CourseMate	
	Web Link	eBook p. 252 or CourseMate	
Optical Discs	Text	p. 253	Know the use of LightScribe technology
Archive Discs	Figure	p. 255	Know how an archive disc works

Continued on next page

Continued from previous page

Topic	Resource	Location	Now you should . . .
Managing Files and Folders; Hard Disks	Labs and Windows Exercises	CourseMate	Know how to use Windows to work with folders, to delete and restore files, and to learn statistics about the hard disk on a computer
TurboTax Online	Web Apps	CourseMate	Know how to use TurboTax Online to print and file a tax return

Safe User, Protected from the Risks in a Digital World

Goal: I would like to take measures to (1) protect my computers, devices, and data from loss, damage, or misuse; (2) minimize or prevent risks associated with using technology; and (3) minimize the environmental impact of using computers and related devices.

Topic	Resource	Location	Now you should . . .
Erasing Hard Disks	Ethics & Issues	p. 241	Be familiar with issues surrounding purchase of used hard disks
Crashes	Text/Figure	p. 244	Know how to avoid a head crash
Maintaining Hard Disk	Text	p. 246	Know ways to maintain a hard disk: Cleanup Disk and Defragment Disk
	Learn How To	pp. 266–267 and CourseMate	
	Labs and Windows Exercises	CourseMate	
Airport Screenings	FAQ	p. 250	Know how to safeguard data during air travel
	FAQ Link	eBook p. 250, or Airport Screening Equipment link, CourseMate	
Cloud Storage	Ethics & Issues	p. 252	Be familiar with privacy issues surrounding cloud storage
	Web Link and Video	eBook p. 252 or CourseMate	
Care for and Clean Discs	Text/Figure and FAQ	pp. 253–254	Know how to care for, clean, and repair an optical disc
	FAQ Link	eBook p. 254, or Cleaning and Repairing Discs link, CourseMate	
Medical Records	Ethics & Issues	p. 259	Be aware of privacy issues surrounding medical records
Encrypting USB	Video	At the Movies, CourseMate	Know how to encrypt files on a USB flash drive
Recycle Bin	Windows Exercises	CourseMate	Know how to recover files from the Recycle Bin

Competent Digital Citizen

Goal: I would like to be knowledgeable and well-informed about computers, mobile devices, and related technology, so that I am digitally literate in my personal and professional use of digital devices.

Topic	Resource	Location	Now you should . . .
Storage Media	Text/Figure	pp. 238–239	Be able to state examples of storage media
Access Time	Text	p. 240	Know what access time measures

Continued on next page

Continued from previous page

Topic	Resource	Location	Now you should . . .
Hard Disk Recording Methods	Text	p. 240	Know the difference between perpendicular and longitudinal recording
	Web Link	eBook p. 240 or CourseMate	
Hard Disk Characteristics and Trends	Text/Figures	pp. 240–243	Be familiar with density, formatting, clusters, cylinders, platters, form factors, disk cache and other hard disk characteristics; how hard disks work; and trends related to hard disks
	FAQ Link	eBook p. 241, or Hard Disk Capacity link, CourseMate	
	FAQ	p. 241	
	Figure 6-6 Animation	p. 243	
Media Life	Figure	p. 258	Know the life expectancies of various media
	Drag and Drop Figure 6-29	eBook p. 258 or CourseMate	
Rosetta Project	Looking Ahead	p. 258	Know about the Rosetta Project's long-term storage
	Link and Video	eBook p. 258 or CourseMate	
Computers in Meteorology	Computer Usage @ Work	p. 260	Know how meteorologists use computers in weather forecasting and to predict storm patterns and paths
	Link and Video	eBook p. 260 or CourseMate	

Future Entrepreneur or Professional in a Digital Society

Goal: As I ponder my future, I envision myself as an entrepreneur or skilled professional using technology to support my business endeavors or job responsibilities. Along the way, I may interact with a variety of computer professionals — or I may just become one myself!

Topic	Resource	Location	Now you should . . .
NAS	Text	p. 244	Know the purpose, features, and costs of network attached storage
	Web Link	eBook p. 244 or CourseMate	
Tape	Text/Figure	p. 257	Know how businesses use tape storage and how it works
Magnetic Stripe Cards and Smart Cards	Text/Figure	p. 257	Know how businesses use magnetic stripe cards and smart cards and how they work
	Ethics & Issues		
	Web Link and Video	eBook p. 257 or CourseMate	
Microfilm, Microfiche	Text/Figure	p. 258	Know the purpose and uses of microfilm and microfiche
Enterprise Storage	Text	pp. 258–259	Know how large businesses store data, information, and programs
Storage Recommendations	Text/Figure	p. 259	Be familiar with storage recommendations for various users
Computer Technician	Exploring Computer Careers	CourseMate	Be familiar with the responsibilities and education required for a computer technician

Preparing for a Test

Visit the Computer Concepts CourseMate at www.cengagebrain.com and then navigate to the Chapter 6 Web Apps resource for this book to prepare for your test.

Does your class use the Computer Concepts CourseMate Web site? If so, prepare for your test by using the Flash Cards, Study Guide, and Practice Test Web apps — available for your smart phone or tablet.

If your class does not use the Computer Concepts CourseMate Web site or you prefer to use your book, you can prepare for the test by doing the Quiz Yourself activities on pages 246, 252, and 260; reading the Chapter Review on pages 262–263, ensuring you know the definitions for the terms on page 263; and completing the Checkpoint exercises on page 264. You also should know the material identified in the Chapter 6 Study Guide that follows.

Chapter 6 Study Guide

This study guide identifies material you should know for the Chapter 6 exam. You may want to write the answers in a notebook, enter them on your digital device, record them into a phone, or highlight them in your book. Choose whichever method helps you remember the best.

1. Differentiate between storage devices and storage media.

2. Define storage capacity. Know the terms and abbreviations used to define storage capacity.

3. Differentiate between writing and reading, with respect to storage media.

4. Describe what access time measures.

5. Describe a hard disk. Differentiate between a fixed disk and a portable disk.

6. Differentiate between longitudinal and perpendicular recording.

7. Describe the purpose of a wiping utility.

8. Describe the characteristics of an internal hard disk including capacity, platters, size, read/write heads, cylinders, sectors and tracks, revolutions per minute, transfer rate, and access time.

9. Explain how a hard disk works.

10. Describe what causes a head crash.

11. Define the term, backup.

12. A group of two or more integrated hard disks is called a(n) _____.

13. Discuss the purpose of network attached storage devices.

14. Differentiate between external hard disks and removable hard disks. Identify their advantages over fixed disks.

15. Identify devices that contain miniature hard disks.

16. Differentiate among hard disk controllers: SATA, EIDE, SCSI, and SAS.

17. Describe the purpose and advantages of solid state drives.

18. Differentiate among various types of memory cards.

19. Describe the function of a card reader/writer.

20. Identify advantages and capacities of USB flash drives.

21. Describe the purpose and shapes of ExpressCard modules.

22. Describe cloud storage, examples of services provided, and reasons to use cloud storage.

23. Describe the characteristics of optical discs.

24. Define LightScribe technology.

25. Identify guidelines for proper care of optical discs.

26. Explain how to clean an optical disc.

27. State the typical storage capacity of a CD. Differentiate among a CD-ROM, a CD-R, and a CD-RW.

28. _____ is the process of writing on an optical disc.

29. Describe ripping, with respect to CDs.

30. Explain the purpose of an archive disc or Picture CD.

31. State the storage capacities of DVDs. Differentiate among DVD-ROMs, recordable DVDs, and rewritable DVDs.

32. Describe features of Blu-ray Discs and drives.

33. Describe tape storage and identify its primary use today.

34. Identify uses of magnetic stripe cards and smart cards.

35. Identify uses of microfilm and microfiche.

36. Order these media in terms of life expectancy, from shortest to longest: optical discs, solid state drives, magnetic disks, and microfilm.

37. Explain why an enterprise's storage needs may change.

38. Describe the types of standards set by HIPAA.

39. Explain how meteorologists use computers to predict the weather.

40. Name the company that has the rights to design, develop, manufacture, and market every type of flash memory card format.

Check This Out

As technology changes, you must keep up with updates, new products, breakthroughs, and recent advances to remain digitally literate. The list below identifies topics related to this chapter that you should explore to keep current. In parentheses beside each topic, you will find a search term to help begin your research using a search engine, such as Google.

1. **largest storage medium capacity** (search for: largest storage medium bytes)
2. **latest hard disk technologies** (search for: latest hard disks)
3. **popular failed hard disk data recovery methods** (search for: hard disk recovery software)
4. **widely used network attached storage devices** (search for: top network attached storage)
5. **new external hard disks** (search for: latest external hard disks)
6. **top removable hard disks** (search for: best removable hard disks)
7. **recent miniature hard disks** (search for: latest mini hard disks)
8. **widely used eSATA hard disk controllers** (search for: eSATA hard disk)
9. **popular solid state drives** (search for: top solid state drives)
10. **widely used memory cards** (search for: popular memory cards)
11. **innovative USB flash drives** (search for: latest USB flash drives)
12. **new ExpressCard modules** (search for: ExpressCard module growth)
13. **cloud storage developments** (search for: cloud storage news)
14. **latest Blu-ray Disc formats** (search for: new Blu-ray disc specifications)
15. **smart card technology advancements** (search for: smart card news)

For current news and information
Check us out on Facebook and Twitter. See your instructor or the Computer Concepts CourseMate for specific information.

Student Success Guide
Operating Systems and Utility Programs

Why Should I Learn About Operating Systems and Utility Programs?

"My computer is running slower than when I bought it, but it seems to be working properly. I installed an antivirus program and update it and my Windows software occasionally. Aside from looking into ways to speed up my computer, why do I need to learn about operating systems and utility programs?"

True, you may be familiar with some of the material in this chapter, but do you know . . .

"Why do I need to learn about operating systems and utility programs?"

- Which combination of characters you should use to create a secure password? (p. 278, FAQ)
- Why a personal firewall may protect against unauthorized intrusions? (p. 287, Personal Firewall)
- What signs may indicate your computer is infected with a virus? (p. 288, Antivirus Programs)
- How e-learning systems may increase your retention and enhance your overall educational experience? (p. 292, Computer Usage @ Work)
- Who developed an operating system when he was a 21-year-old computer science student in Finland? (p. 293, Technology Trailblazers)
- How to update Windows regularly? (p. 298–299 and Computer Concepts CourseMate, Learn How To)
- How Windows can back up and restore files? (Windows Exercises, Computer Concepts CourseMate)
- How to purchase a desktop or notebook computer, smart phone, portable media player, and digital camera? (p. 301–312, Buyer's Guide Special Feature)

For these answers and to discover much more information essential to this course, read Chapter 7 and visit the associated Computer Concepts CourseMate at www.cengagebrain.com.

Q & A How can I meet one or more of these goals?

Make use of the goal's resources for each chapter in the book and you should meet that goal by the end of the course.

Customize Your Learning Experience

Adapt this book to meet your needs by determining your goal. Would you like to be an informed digital consumer? A productive technology user? A safe user, protected from the risks in a digital world? A competent digital citizen? A future entrepreneur or professional in a digital society?

Every chapter in this Student Success Guide identifies resources targeted toward each of these goals, along with criteria to verify you understand the resources' content. Resources may be located in the textbook, on the Computer Concepts CourseMate Web site, in the interactive eBook, and on the Web.

Informed Digital Consumer

Goal: I would like to understand the terminology used in Web or print advertisements that sell computers, mobile devices, and related technology, as well as the jargon used by sales associates in computer or electronics stores, so that I can make informed purchasing decisions.

Topic	Resource	Location	Now you should . . .
Platform	Text	p. 272	Know the meaning of a required platform on a software package
Aero Interface	Text/Figure	p. 273	Know RAM requirements for Windows Aero vs. Windows 7 Basic
Embedded Operating Systems	Text/Figure	p. 283	Know the features of embedded operating systems: Windows Embedded CE, Windows Phone, Palm OS, iPhone OS, Blackberry, Google Android, Embedded Linux, and Symbian OS

Continued on next page

Continued from previous page

Topic	Resource	Location	Now you should . . .
File Compression	Text	p. 290	Know the purpose of file compression utilities and popular programs
	Web Link	eBook p. 290 or CourseMate	Be familiar with WinZip
Media Players	Text/Figure	p. 290	Know the purpose of media players and popular players
Disc Burning	Text/Figure	p. 291	Know the purpose of disc burning software
Personal Computers	Text/Figure	p. 291	Know the purpose of personal computer maintenance utilities
RIM	Text	p. 293	Be familiar with RIM's products and services
	Link	eBook p. 293 or CourseMate	
Buyer's Guide	Text/Figures	pp. 301–312	Know some considerations when purchasing a desktop computer, notebook computer, smart phone, portable media player, and digital camera
	Drag and Drop Figure 7-2	eBook pp. 303–304 or CourseMate	
	Videos	eBook p. 300, 306, 309, and 311 or CourseMate	
	Links	eBook p. 312 or CourseMate	

Productive Technology User

Goal: I would like to learn ways that technology can benefit me at home, work, and school. I also would like to learn helpful techniques for using technology so that I can perform tasks more efficiently and be more productive in daily activities.

Topic	Resource	Location	Now you should . . .
Starting and Shutting Down a Computer	Text/Figure	p. 272	Know how to perform a cold boot, warm boot, restart, and shut down options
	Drag and Drop Figure 7-2	eBook p. 272 or CourseMate	
Foreground Program	Text/Figure	p. 274	Know how to make a program active (in the foreground)
Plug and Play	Text	p. 276	Know how Plug and Play works
Network Connections	Text/Figure	p. 276	Know how to connect to a network using Windows
Performance	Text	p. 277	Know how to monitor performance using Windows
Automatic Update	Text	p. 277	Know the benefits of using automatic update
Passwords	Text/Figure and FAQ	p. 278	Know how to select a good password
	FAQ Link	eBook p. 278, or Passwords link, CourseMate	
Windows	Text/Figure	p. 278	Know some features and editions of Windows 7
	Web Link	eBook p. 278 or CourseMate	
	Figure Video		
	Windows Exercises	CourseMate	Know how to determine the Windows version on a computer
	Learn How To	pp. 298–299 and CourseMate	Know how to keep Windows up-to-date
Mac OS X	Text/Figure	p. 281	Know some features of Mac OS X
	Link and Video	eBook p. 281 or CourseMate	
UNIX	Text/Figure	p. 281	Know some features of UNIX

Continued on next page

Continued from previous page

Topic	Resource	Location	Now you should . . .
Linux	Text/Figure	p. 282	Know some features of Linux
	Web Link	eBook p. 282 or CourseMate	
File Manager	Text/Figure	p. 285	Know the purpose of a file manager
Search Utility	Text/Figure	p. 285	Know the purpose of a search utility
Uninstaller	Text	p. 285	Know the purpose of an uninstaller and how to delete a program properly
	Labs	CourseMate	
Image Viewer	Text/Figure	p. 285	Know the purpose of an image viewer
Disk Cleanup	Text	p. 286	Know the purpose of a disk cleanup utility
Disk Defragmenter	Text/Figure	p. 286	Know the purpose of a disk defragmenter utility
	Figure 7-18 Animation	eBook p. 286 or CourseMate	
Backup and Restore	Text	p. 286	Know the purpose of a backup and a restore utility and how to use Windows Backup and Restore
	Windows Exercises	CourseMate	
Screen Saver	Text	p. 287	Know the purpose of a screen saver and how to use one
	Windows Exercises	CourseMate	
Burning Video Discs	Learn How To	p. 298 and CourseMate	Know how to use Windows Explorer to burn a disc
Verisign	Text	p. 293	Be familiar with Verisign's services
	Link	eBook p. 293 or CourseMate	
Install and Maintain	Link	Book-Level Resource, CourseMate	Be familiar with how to install and maintain a computer
Photo Editing	Web Apps	CourseMate	Know how to use Photoshop Express to upload, edit, and share photos

Safe User, Protected from the Risks in a Digital World

Goal: I would like to take measures to (1) protect my computers, devices, and data from loss, damage, or misuse; (2) minimize or prevent risks associated with using technology; and (3) minimize the environmental impact of using computers and related devices.

Topic	Resource	Location	Now you should . . .
Recover Deleted Files	Innovative Computing	p. 284	Be familiar with utilities that enable you to recover deleted files
	Link and Video	eBook p. 284 or CourseMate	
Personal Firewall	Text/Figure	p. 287	Know how a personal firewall can protect your computer
Antivirus Programs	Text/Figures	pp. 288–289	Know how antivirus programs protect your computer
Computer Viruses	FAQ	p. 288	Recognize signs of virus infection and steps to prevent computer virus infection
	FAQ Link	eBook p. 288, or Virus Infections link, CourseMate	
	Video	At the Movies, CourseMate	
	Labs	CourseMate	

Continued on next page

Continued from previous page

Topic	Resource	Location	Now you should . . .
Spyware Removers	Text	p. 289	Know the purpose of spyware and adware removers
Internet Filters	Text and FAQ	pp. 289–290	Know the purpose of anti-spam programs, Web filters, phishing filters, and pop-up blockers
	FAQ Link	eBook p. 289, or Spam link, CourseMate	

Competent Digital Citizen

Goal: I would like to be knowledgeable and well-informed about computers, mobile devices, and related technology, so that I am digitally literate in my personal and professional use of digital devices.

Topic	Resource	Location	Now you should . . .
System Software	Text	p. 270	Know the definition of system software
Start Up Process	Text	p. 272	Be able to describe what occurs when you boot up a personal computer
Command Language	Text	p. 273	Know the purpose of a command-line interface
Program Management	Text/Figures	pp. 273–274	Know various ways an operating system can handle programs
Virtual Memory	Text	p. 275	Know how a computer might use virtual memory
Spooling and Drivers	Text/Figure	pp. 275–276	Know how buffers and spooling work and the purpose of drivers
Eye Monitor	Looking Ahead	p. 277	Be familiar with a health-based performance monitor
	Link and Video	eBook p. 277 or CourseMate	
Operating Systems	Text/Figure	p. 279	Know examples of operating systems in each category: stand-alone, server, and embedded
	Drag and Drop Figure 7-8	eBook p. 279 or CourseMate	
Open vs. Closed Source	Ethics & Issues	p. 282	Be familiar with the issues around open and closed source programs
	Video	eBook p. 282 or CourseMate	
Computers in Education	Computer Usage @ Work	p. 292	Recognize how students and instructors use computers in school
	Link and Video	eBook p. 292 or CourseMate	
Steve Wozniak	Text	p. 293	Be familiar with Steve Wozniak's impact on the computing industry
	Link and Video	eBook p. 293 or CourseMate	
Linus Torvalds	Text	p. 293	Be familiar with Linus Torvald's role with operating systems
	Link	eBook p. 293 or CourseMate	

Future Entrepreneur or Professional in a Digital Society

Goal: As I ponder my future, I envision myself as an entrepreneur or skilled professional using technology to support my business endeavors or job responsibilities. Along the way, I may interact with a variety of computer professionals — or I may just become one myself!

Topic	Resource	Location	Now you should . . .
Network Admin.	Text	p. 278	Know the role of a network administrator
Operating Systems	FAQ	p. 279	Know the market shares of various operating systems
	FAQ Link	eBook p. 279, or Operating System Market Share link, CourseMate	

Continued on next page

Continued from previous page

Topic	Resource	Location	Now you should . . .
Server Operating Systems	Text	pp. 282–283	Be familiar with Windows Server, UNIX, Linus, Solaris, and NetWare
Systems Programmer	Exploring Computer Careers	CourseMate	Be familiar with the responsibilities and education required for a systems programmer

Preparing for a Test

Visit the Computer Concepts CourseMate at www.cengagebrain.com and then navigate to the Chapter 7 Web Apps resource for this book to prepare for your test.

Does your class use the Computer Concepts CourseMate Web site? If so, prepare for your test by using the Flash Cards, Study Guide, and Practice Test Web apps — available for your smart phone or tablet.

If your class does not use the Computer Concepts CourseMate Web site or you prefer to use your book, you can prepare for the test by doing the Quiz Yourself activities on pages 279, 284, and 292; reading the Chapter Review on pages 294–295; ensuring you know the definitions for the terms on page 295; and completing the Checkpoint exercises on page 296. You also should know the material identified in the Chapter 7 Study Guide that follows.

Chapter 7 Study Guide

This study guide identifies material you should know for the Chapter 7 exam. You may want to write the answers in a notebook, enter them on your digital device, record them into a phone, or highlight them in your book. Choose whichever method helps you remember the best.

1. Define the term, system software. Identify the two types of system software.

2. Define the term, operating system.

3. Define the terms, platform and cross-platform.

4. _____ is the process of starting or restarting a computer.

5. Differentiate a cold boot from a warm boot.

6. Define the term, kernel.

7. Describe various shut down options: powering off, sleep mode, and hibernate.

8. Describe the purpose of a user interface. Differentiate between a GUI and command-line interface.

9. In relation to operating systems, explain the difference between single user/single tasking, single user/multitasking, multiuser, and multiprocessing.

10. Differentiate between foreground and background.

11. Describe how an operating system manages memory.

12. Describe virtual memory.

13. Explain how an operating system coordinates tasks or jobs.

14. Define the term, buffer. Explain how spooling uses buffers and a queue.

15. Define the term, driver. Explain how the operating system uses drivers and the role of Plug and Play.

16. Describe the purpose of a performance monitor.

17. _____ is a term that means computer error.

18. Briefly explain the types of updates that occur in an automatic update.

19. Describe a server operating system.

20. Describe the role of a network administrator. Differentiate administrator account from user account.

21. Define the terms, user name and password. Identify guidelines for selecting a good password.

22. Explain the reason for encryption.

23. Differentiate among a stand-alone operating system, a server operating system, and an embedded operating system.

24. Summarize the features of these stand-alone operating systems: Windows, Mac OS, UNIX, and Linux.

25. State advantages of open source software.

26. Name examples of server operating systems.

27. Briefly describe and identify uses of these embedded operating systems: Windows Embedded CE, Windows Phone, iPhone OS, BlackBerry, and Google Android.

28. Explain how it is possible to recover a deleted file.

29. Describe the purpose of a file manager, search utility, uninstaller, image viewer, and disk cleanup utility.

30. Describe the purpose of a disk defragmenter. Describe why a fragmented disk is slower than one that is defragmented.

31. Describe the purpose of a backup and restore utility, screen saver, and personal firewall.

Continued on next page

Continued from previous page

32. Define computer virus. Identify signs of a virus infection. Describe the purpose of an antivirus program.

33. Describe the purpose of spyware and adware removers, anti-spam programs, Web filters, phishing filters, pop-up blockers, file compression utilities, media players, disc burning software, and personal computer maintenance utilities.

34. Explain the use of e-learning systems.

35. RIM's key product is its _____ smart phone.

36. _____ cofounded Apple with Steve Jobs.

37. Linus Torvalds created the open source operating system called _____.

38. Briefly describe some considerations when purchasing a desktop computer, notebook computer, smart phone, portable media player, and digital camera.

Check This Out

As technology changes, you must keep up with updates, new products, breakthroughs, and recent advances to remain digitally literate. The list below identifies topics related to this chapter that you should explore to keep current. In parentheses beside each topic, you will find a search term to help begin your research using a search engine, such as Google.

For current news and information
Check us out on Facebook and Twitter. See your instructor or the Computer Concepts CourseMate for specific information.

1. largest operating system market share (search for: top market share operating systems)

2. features of latest Windows operating system (search for: latest Microsoft Windows features)

3. features of newest Apple OS operating system (search for: latest Macintosh OS features)

4. recent UNIX operating system elements (search for: new UNIX features)

5. new Linux GUI enhancements (search for: Linux GUI)

6. latest Windows Server edition (search for: recent Windows Server)

7. recent Windows Phone operating system (search for: latest Windows mobile OS)

8. new iPhone and iPad OS features (search for: iOS news)

9. popular utility software (search for: best utility programs)

10. best utilities to back up data (search for: backup utilities review)

11. top antivirus programs (search for: popular antivirus software)

12. widely used spyware removal programs (search for: popular spyware programs)

13. popular e-learning management systems (search for: top e-learning software)

14. updates about Steve Wozniak's projects (search for: Steve Wozniak news)

15. latest guidelines for purchasing computers (search for: computer buying guide)

Communications and Networks

Chapter 8

Why Should I Learn About Communications and Networks?

"I use my new smart phone to send text messages, send and receive voice mail, and navigate using a GPS app. At home, I have a broadband Internet connection, and I also access the Internet wirelessly at local hot spots or anywhere on campus. What more do I need to learn about communications and networks?"

True, you may be familiar with some of the material in this chapter, but do you know . . .

"What more do I need to learn about communications and networks?"

- How to use your GPS to find hidden treasure? (p. 321, Innovative Computing)
- Why you can participate in online meetings with collaboration software? (p. 321, Collaboration)
- How you are able to access your school network wirelessly? (p. 355, Wireless Access Points)
- Why you should be concerned about radiation from your cell phone and other devices? (p. 340, Ethics & Issues)
- How the agriculture industry uses computers to help grow crops? (p. 342, Computer Usage @ Work)
- Which communications company's name is derived from the Roman goddess of truth? (p. 343, Companies on the Cutting Edge)
- How to set up and install a Wi-Fi home network? (p. 348 and Computer Concepts CourseMate, Learn How To)
- How to view Windows Firewall security settings? (Windows Exercises, Computer Concepts CourseMate)

For these answers and to discover much more information essential to this course, read Chapter 8 and visit the associated Computer Concepts CourseMate at www.cengagebrain.com.

Customize Your Learning Experience

Q&A How can I meet one or more of these goals?

Make use of the goal's resources for each chapter in the book and you should meet that goal by the end of the course.

Adapt this book to meet your needs by determining your goal. Would you like to be an informed digital consumer? A productive technology user? A safe user, protected from the risks in a digital world? A competent digital citizen? A future entrepreneur or professional in a digital society?

Every chapter in this Student Success Guide identifies resources targeted toward each of these goals, along with criteria to verify you understand the resources' content. Resources may be located in the textbook, on the Computer Concepts CourseMate Web site, in the interactive eBook, and on the Web.

Informed Digital Consumer

Goal: I would like to understand the terminology used in Web or print advertisements that sell computers, mobile devices, and related technology, as well as the jargon used by sales associates in computer or electronics stores, so that I can make informed purchasing decisions.

Topic	Resource	Location	Now you should . . .
Internet Connections	Text/Figure	pp. 331–332	Be aware of costs and transfer rates of various Internet connections
	Drag and Drop Figure 8-16	eBook p. 332 or CourseMate	

Continued on next page

Continued from previous page

Topic	Resource	Location	Now you should . . .
Modems	Text/Figures and FAQ	pp. 333–334	Know the purpose and uses of various modem types: dial-up modems, digital modems (ISDN, DSL, and cable), and wireless modems
	FAQ Link	eBook p. 334, or Cable Internet Service link, CourseMate	
Network Cards	Text/Figure	p. 334	Know the purpose and styles of network cards
Wireless Access Point	Text/Figure	p. 335	Know the purpose of a wireless access point
Routers	Text/Figure	p. 335	Know the purpose of routers
Mobile TV	Links and Video	eBook p. 341 or CourseMate	Be familiar with how to watch live programs on a computer or mobile device
	Video	At the Movies, CourseMate	
Verizon	Text	p. 343	Be familiar with Verizon's products and services
	Link	eBook p. 343 or CourseMate	

Productive Technology User

Goal: I would like to learn ways that technology can benefit me at home, work, and school. I also would like to learn helpful techniques for using technology so that I can perform tasks more efficiently and be more productive in daily activities.

Topic	Resource	Location	Now you should . . .
Uses of Computer Communications	Text/Figure	pp. 315–316	Know the uses of computer communications previously discussed
	Drag and Drop Figure 8-2	eBook p. 316 or CourseMate	
	Web Link		
Wireless Messaging	Text/Figure and FAQ	pp. 316–318	Know the guidelines and uses of text, picture/video, and wireless instant messaging
	Figure Video	eBook p. 317 or CourseMate	
	FAQ and Web Link		
Wireless Internet Access Points	Text/Figure	pp. 318–319	Be familiar with hot spots and mobile wireless networks
Cybercafés	Text	p. 319	Know the services offered by cybercafés
GPS	Text/Figure	p. 320	Know how GPS works, and name devices with GPS capability
	Web Link	eBook p. 320 or CourseMate	
Voice Mail	Text	p. 322	Know how voice mail and visual voice mail work
Internet Peer-to-Peer	Text/Figure	p. 326	Know the uses of a file sharing or P2P network
	Web Link	eBook p. 326 or CourseMate	
Wi-Fi	Text	p. 329	Know the purpose and uses of Wi-Fi and hot spots
Bluetooth, UWB, IrDA	Text	pp. 480–481	Know the uses of Bluetooth, UWB, and IrDA communications
Communications Software	Text	pp. 330–331	Know the purpose of communications software

Continued on next page

Continued from previous page

Topic	Resource	Location	Now you should . . .
Internet Connections	Text/Figures	pp. 331–332	Know the how these Internet connections work: dial-up, ISDN, DSL, FTTP, T-carrier, and ATM
Home Networks	Text	pp. 336–337	Know the benefits of a home network, the types of wired and wireless home networks, and how to set up a home network
	Web Link	eBook p. 336 or CourseMate	
	Figure 8-21 Animation		
	Learn How To	pp. 348–349 and CourseMate	
Modems and Network Connections	Windows Exercises	CourseMate	Know how to use Windows to learn about the modem connected to a computer and view the computer's network connections
Gmail	Web Apps	CourseMate	Know how to use Gmail to send and receive e-mail messages

Safe User, Protected from the Risks in a Digital World

Goal: I would like to take measures to (1) protect my computers, devices, and data from loss, damage, or misuse; (2) minimize or prevent risks associated with using technology; and (3) minimize the environmental impact of using computers and related devices.

Topic	Resource	Location	Now you should . . .
Cellular and Wi-Fi Radiation	Ethics & Issues	p. 340	Know about potential health effects from cell phones, cellular antennas, and Wi-Fi devices
Wireless Security	Labs	CourseMate	Be familiar with ways to secure an access point
Windows Firewall	Windows Exercises	CourseMate	Be familiar with how to use Windows Firewall

Competent Digital Citizen

Goal: I would like to be knowledgeable and well-informed about computers, mobile devices, and related technology, so that I am digitally literate in my personal and professional use of digital devices.

Topic	Resource	Location	Now you should . . .
Communications	Text/Figure	pp. 314–315	Know the components required in a communications system
Print Media	Ethics & Issues	p. 318	Be aware of the impact of high-speed broadband on print media
Geocaching	Innovative Computing	p. 321	Be familiar with how geocaching uses GPS technology
	Link and Video	eBook p. 321 or CourseMate	
Body Area Network	Looking Ahead	p. 323	Be familiar with the uses of body area networks
	Link and Video	eBook p. 323 or CourseMate	
LANs, MANs, WANs	Text/Figures	pp. 323–324	Know the differences among LANs, MANs, and WANs
	Labs	CourseMate	
WAP	Text	p. 330	Know the uses of WAP
Communications Channel	Text/Figure	pp. 337–338	Know the meaning of bandwidth and latency, and the types of transmission media used on a communications channel

Continued on next page

Continued from previous page

Topic	Resource	Location	Now you should . . .
Physical Transmission Media	Text/Figures	pp. 339–340	Be familiar with the composition of twisted-pair cable, coaxial cable, and fiber-optic cable
	Drag and Drop Figures 8-24 and 8-25	eBook pp. 339–340 or CourseMate	
Wireless Transmission Media	Text	pp. 340–341	Be familiar with technologies used in infrared, broadcast radio, cellular radio, microwaves, and communications satellite
Computers in Agriculture	Computer Usage @ Work	p. 342	Recognize how computers are used in the agriculture industry
	Link and Video	eBook p. 342 or CourseMate	
Network Communications	Text	p. 343	Recognize that data in a network flows through several layers
	Link and Video	eBook p. 343 or CourseMate	
Cisco	Text	p. 343	Be familiar with Cisco's products and services
	Link and Video	eBook p. 343 or CourseMate	
Robert Metcalf	Text	p. 343	Be familiar with Robert Metcalf's impact on network communications
	Link and Video	eBook p. 343 or CourseMate	

Future Entrepreneur or Professional in a Digital Society

Goal: As I ponder my future, I envision myself as an entrepreneur or skilled professional using technology to support my business endeavors or job responsibilities. Along the way, I may interact with a variety of computer professionals — or I may just become one myself!

Topic	Resource	Location	Now you should . . .
Collaboration	Text/Figure	p. 321	Be familiar with collaboration tools: collaborative software and document management systems
Groupware	Text	pp. 321–322	Be familiar with the benefits of groupware in business
Web Services	Text	p. 322	Know the purpose of Web services in business
Network Advantages	Text	p. 322	Know the reasons businesses use networks
Network Architectures	Text/Figures	pp. 325–326	Know the difference between client/server and peer-to-peer networks
Network Topologies	Text/Figures	pp. 326–327	Know the differences among star, bus, and ring networks
Intranets	Text	p. 328	Know how businesses use Intranets and extranets
Ethernet, Token Ring, TCP/IP	Text	p. 329	Be able to differentiate among the Ethernet, token ring, and TCP/IP network communications standards
RFID	Text/Figure	p. 330	Know how RFID works and its uses
	Web Link	eBook p. 330 or CourseMate	
WiMAX	Text	p. 330	Know the purpose and uses of WiMAX
Network Specialist	Exploring Computer Careers	CourseMate	Be familiar with the responsibilities and education required for a network specialist

Preparing for a Test

Visit the Computer Concepts CourseMate at www.cengagebrain.com and then navigate to the Chapter 8 Web Apps resource for this book to prepare for your test.

Does your class use the Computer Concepts CourseMate Web site? If so, prepare for your test by using the Flash Cards, Study Guide, and Practice Test Web apps — available for your smart phone or tablet.

If your class does not use the Computer Concepts CourseMate Web site or you prefer to use your book, you can prepare for the test by doing the Quiz Yourself activities on pages 322, 333, and 342; reading the Chapter Review on pages 344–345; ensuring you know the definitions for the terms on page 345; and completing the Checkpoint exercises on page 346. You also should know the material identified in the Chapter 8 Study Guide that follows.

Chapter 8 Study Guide

This study guide identifies material you should know for the Chapter 8 exam. You may want to write the answers in a notebook, enter them on your digital device, record them into a phone, or highlight them in your book. Choose whichever method helps you remember the best.

1. Define computer communications.

2. Discuss the purpose of the components required for successful communications: sending device, communications device, communications channel, and receiving device.

3. Identify various sending and receiving devices.

4. Briefly describe these communications: blogs, chat rooms, e-mail, fax, FTP, instant messaging, Internet, RSS, video conferencing, VoIP, Web, Web 2.0, and wikis.

5. A synonym for text messaging is _____.

6. Describe text messaging.

7. Describe picture messaging and video messaging.

8. A synonym for picture/video messaging is _____.

9. Define wireless Internet access point.

10. Define hot spot. Describe three hot spot technologies.

11. Describe a mobile wireless network.

12. Describe a cybercafé.

13. GPS stands for _____. Give examples of GPS receivers. Cite uses of GPS technology.

14. Explain geocaching.

15. Describe uses of these computer communications: collaboration, groupware, voice mail, and Web services.

16. Define the term, network. List advantages of using a network.

17. Describe how sensors might work in a body area network (BAN). Identify potential uses of BANs.

18. Differentiate among LANs, MANs, and WANs.

19. A server sometimes is called a(n) _____ computer. State examples of dedicated servers.

20. Differentiate between client/server and peer-to-peer networks.

21. Describe how a P2P network works.

22. Differentiate among a star network, bus network, and ring network.

23. Describe how an intranet works. Identify the relationship of an extranet to an intranet.

24. Describe the purpose of network standards and protocols.

25. Differentiate among the Ethernet, token ring, and TCP/IP standards.

26. Describe the Wi-Fi standard. Name some uses of Wi-Fi.

27. Describe the Bluetooth standard. Give examples of some Bluetooth devices.

28. Briefly describe UWB and IrDA standards.

29. RFID stands for _____. Explain how RFID works.

30. Describe the WiMAX standard.

31. Explain the purpose of communications software.

32. Describe various types of lines for communications over the telephone network: dial-up, ISDN, DSL, FTTP, T-carrier, and ATM.

33. Differentiate a dial-up modem from a digital modem. Explain differences between ISDN modems, DSL modems, and cable modems.

34. Describe the purpose of wireless modems and network cards. Identify types of each.

35. State the purpose of a wireless access point and a router. Explain security features built-in some routers.

36. Describe the advantages of a home network. Discuss different wired and wireless ways to set up a home network.

37. Define the term, bandwidth.

38. Describe the purpose of transmission media. Define the term, broadband media.

39. Define noise, as it relates to computer communications.

Continued on next page

Continued from previous page

40. Describe characteristics of these physical transmission media: twisted-pair cable, coaxial cable, and fiber-optic cable.

41. Describe characteristics of these wireless transmission media: infrared, broadcast radio, cellular radio, microwaves, and communications satellite.

42. Cisco manufactures _____ equipment.

43. Identify products and services by Verizon.

44. Robert Metcalfe invented the _____ standard for computer communications.

Check This Out

As technology changes, you must keep up with updates, new products, breakthroughs, and recent advances to remain digitally literate. The list below identifies topics related to this chapter that you should explore to keep current. In parentheses beside each topic, you will find a search term to help begin your research using a search engine, such as Google.

1. **news of using a cell phone as a primary telephone** (search for: cell phone primary phone)

2. **latest developments of working securely from a hot spot** (search for: wireless security hot spot)

3. **recent company use of GPS applications for tracking** (search for: GPS tracking system)

4. **recent geocaching developments** (search for: new geocaching adventures)

5. **popular online groupware applications** (search for: best groupware reviews)

6. **new document management systems for collaboration** (search for: electronic document management software)

7. **widely used mashups** (search for: best mashups)

8. **latest electronic funds transfers using cell phones** (search for: cell phone transfer funds news)

9. **popular wireless LAN devices** (search for: best wireless LAN hardware)

10. **recent software to monitor Internet use** (search for: Internet usage control)

11. **widely used network communications standards** (search for: network communications standards reviews)

12. **Wi-Fi Internet access developments** (search for: new Wi-Fi Internet technology)

13. **popular Bluetooth products** (search for: top Bluetooth devices)

14. **latest digital modems** (search for: digital modem news)

15. **useful advice for creating a wireless home network** (search for: wireless home network guide)

For current news and information
Check us out on Facebook and Twitter. See your instructor or the Computer Concepts CourseMate for specific information.

Why Should I Learn About Database Management?

"I realize my school maintains data about me on its computer system, including my contact information, schedule, and grades. At home, I use my computer to keep track of my income and expenses. I also have a list of repairs and modifications I have made to the car I am restoring. So, why do I need to learn about managing databases?"

True, you may be familiar with some of the material in this chapter, but do you know . . .

"Why do I need to learn about managing databases?"

- Why your privacy may be compromised when your personal data is stored in Internet databases? (p. 354, Ethics & Issues)
- How holograms authenticate Major League Baseball items? (p. 359, Innovative Computing)
- What action you should take if you accidentally discover a file with private data on a publically accessible area of the Internet? (p. 367, Ethics & Issues)
- Why your playlists are kept in a database? (p. 369, FAQ)
- How databases automate processes in the health care industry? (p. 372, Computer Usage @ Work)
- Who developed the relational database design structure that is used for most databases used today? (p. 373, Technology Trailblazers)
- How to organize files using folders? (p. 378 and Computer Concepts CourseMate, Learn How To)
- How to manage folders on a storage device? (Windows Exercises, Computer Concepts CourseMate)

For these answers and to discover much more information essential to this course, read Chapter 9 and visit the associated Computer Concepts CourseMate at www.cengagebrain.com.

Q&A | How can I meet one or more of these goals?

Make use of the goal's resources for each chapter in the book and you should meet that goal by the end of the course.

Customize Your Learning Experience

Adapt this book to meet your needs by determining your goal. Would you like to be an informed digital consumer? A productive technology user? A safe user, protected from the risks in a digital world? A competent digital citizen? A future entrepreneur or professional in a digital society?

Every chapter in this Student Success Guide identifies resources targeted toward each of these goals, along with criteria to verify you understand the resources' content. Resources may be located in the textbook, on the Computer Concepts CourseMate Web site, in the interactive eBook, and on the Web.

Informed Digital Consumer

Goal: I would like to understand the terminology used in Web or print advertisements that sell computers, mobile devices, and related technology, as well as the jargon used by sales associates in computer or electronics stores, so that I can make informed purchasing decisions.

Topic	Resource	Location	Now you should . . .
DBMSs	Figure	p. 363	Know popular DBMSs
	Web Link	eBook p. 363 or CourseMate	
Database Vendors	FAQ	p. 363	Know market share of database vendors
Data Models and Terminology	Text	p. 368	Know the various data models and data terminology used in file processing and relational database environments
	Drag and Drop Figure 9-16	eBook p. 368 or CourseMate	

Productive Technology User

Goal: I would like to learn ways that technology can benefit me at home, work, and school. I also would like to learn helpful techniques for using technology so that I can perform tasks more efficiently and be more productive in daily activities.

Topic	Resource	Location	Now you should . . .
Information	Text	p. 354	Know the qualities of valuable information for decision making
Adding Records	Text/Figure	p. 357	Be familiar with reasons for and process of adding records to a file
Modifying Records	Text/Figure	pp. 357–358	Be familiar with reasons for and process of modifying records in a file
Deleting Records	Text/Figure	pp. 358–359	Be familiar with reasons for and process of deleting records in a file
Data Dictionary	Text/Figure	p. 364	Be familiar with the use of a data dictionary
	Drag and Drop Figure 9-12	eBook p. 364 or CourseMate	
File Retrieval and Maintenance	Text/Figures	pp. 364–366	Be familiar with the use of query languages, query by example, forms, and report generators
	Drag and Drop Figure 9-13	eBook p. 365 or CourseMate	
SQL	Text/Figure	p. 369	Be familiar with SQL
	Link and Video	eBook p. 364 or CourseMate	
Employee as a User	Text	p. 372	Know how employees uses databases
Photo Sharing Site	Video	At the Movies, CourseMate	Know how a photo sharing site keeps its data
Spreadsheets	Labs	CourseMate	Be familiar with advanced uses of spreadsheets
Databases	Labs	CourseMate	Be familiar with advanced uses of databases
Files and Folders	Learn How To	pp. 378–379 and CourseMate	Know how to use Windows to manage, organize, and search for files and folders
	Windows Exercises		
Calendar	Web Apps	CourseMate	Know how to use Windows Live Calendar

Safe User, Protected from the Risks in a Digital World

Goal: I would like to take measures to (1) protect my computers, devices, and data from loss, damage, or misuse; (2) minimize or prevent risks associated with using technology; and (3) minimize the environmental impact of using computers and related devices.

Topic	Resource	Location	Now you should . . .
Privacy	Ethics & Issues	p. 354	Realize privacy issues associated with Internet databases
Data Security	Text	p. 367	Be familiar with the levels of access privileges
Backup and Recovery	Text	p. 367	Know the purpose of a backup, a log, a recovery utility, and continuous backup
Security Breaches	Ethics & Issues	p. 370	Know the privacy issues surrounding database security
	Video	eBook p. 370 or CourseMate	

Competent Digital Citizen

Goal: I would like to be knowledgeable and well-informed about computers, mobile devices, and related technology, so that I am digitally literate in my personal and professional use of digital devices.

Topic	Resource	Location	Now you should . . .
Databases	Text	pp. 352–353	Know the purpose of a database and database software, and how database software is used to process data into information
	Figure 9-1 Animation	eBook p. 352 or CourseMate	
Data Integrity	Text	p. 353	Understand the importance of data integrity
Hierarchy of Data	Text/Figures	pp. 355–356	Know the difference between characters, fields, records, and files; know data types of fields
	Drag and Drop Figure 9-2	p. 355	
Baseball Databases	Innovative Computing	p. 359	Know how databases are used in baseball memorabilia authentication and online baseball games
	Link and Video	eBook p. 359 or CourseMate	
DNA Barcoding	Looking Ahead	p. 365	Be familiar with how databases are used to catalog species of plants, animals, and microbes
	Link and Video	eBook p. 365 or CourseMate	
Relational Databases	Text/Figure	pp. 368–369	Know the organization and uses of relational databases
Object-Oriented Databases	Text/Figure	p. 369	Know the organization and uses of object-oriented databases
Portable Media Player	FAQ	p. 369	Know how portable media players use databases
	FAQ Link	eBook p. 369, or Media Player Databases link, CourseMate	
Multidimensional Databases	Text	p. 370	Know the organization and uses of multidimensional databases
Web Databases	Text/Figure	pp. 370–371	Be familiar with uses and operation of Web databases
E. F. Codd	Text	p. 373	Be familiar with E. F. Codd's impact on relational databases
	Link	eBook p. 373 or CourseMate	
Larry Ellison	Text	p. 373	Be familiar with Larry Ellison's impact on relational databases
	Link and Video	eBook p. 373 or CourseMate	

Future Entrepreneur or Professional in a Digital Society

Goal: As I ponder my future, I envision myself as an entrepreneur or skilled professional using technology to support my business endeavors or job responsibilities. Along the way, I may interact with a variety of computer professionals — or I may just become one myself!

Topic	Resource	Location	Now you should . . .
Data Validation	Text/Figure	pp. 359–360	Know the various checks programmers use to validate data
	Web Link	eBook p. 360 or CourseMate	
File Processing System	Text	p. 361	Be familiar with how organizations use file processing systems and potential disadvantages
Database Approach	Text/Figures and FAQ	pp. 361–362	Be familiar with how organizations uses a database approach and potential benefits over file processing systems
	Drag and Drop Figure 9-10	eBook p. 362 or CourseMate	
Data Warehouses	Text	p. 370	Know how organizations use data warehouses
Database Design Guidelines	Text	p. 371	Be familiar with guidelines for database design
	Web Link	eBook p. 371 or CourseMate	
Database Analysts and Administrators	Text	p. 371	Know the role of database analysts and administrators, and be familiar with responsibilities and education required for database administrators
	Exploring Computer Careers	CourseMate	
Health Sciences	Computer Usage @ Work	p. 372	Know how professionals in the health sciences field use computers to support their activities
	Link and Video	eBook p. 372 or CourseMate	
Oracle	Text	p. 373	Be familiar with Oracle's enterprise products and services
	Link	eBook p. 373 or CourseMate	
Sybase	Text	p. 373	Be familiar with Sybase's enterprise products and services
	Link	eBook p. 373 or CourseMate	

Preparing for a Test

Visit the Computer Concepts CourseMate at www.cengagebrain.com and then navigate to the Chapter 9 Web Apps resource for this book to prepare for your test.

Does your class use the Computer Concepts CourseMate Web site? If so, prepare for your test by using the Flash Cards, Study Guide, and Practice Test Web apps — available for your smart phone or tablet.

If your class does not use the Computer Concepts CourseMate Web site or you prefer to use your book, you can prepare for the test by doing the Quiz Yourself activities on pages 360, 367, and 372; reading the Chapter Review on pages 374–375; ensuring you know the definitions for the terms on page 375; and completing the Checkpoint exercises on page 376. You also should know the material identified in the Chapter 9 Study Guide that follows.

Chapter 9 Study Guide

This study guide identifies material you should know for the Chapter 9 exam. You may want to write the answers in a notebook, enter them on your digital device, record them into a phone, or highlight them in your book. Choose whichever method helps you remember the best.

1. Define database. Explain the purpose of a database management system (DBMS).

2. Explain the meaning of data integrity.

3. GIGO stands for _____. Describe the meaning of this term.

4. Describe seven qualities of valuable information.

5. Order these terms from smallest to largest: records, characters, files, fields. Define and give an example for each term.

6. Identify common data types.

7. Define file maintenance.

8. Identify reasons these activities are performed: adding records to a file, modifying records in a file, and deleting records from a file.

9. Describe ways DBMSs manage deleted records.

10. Explain the purpose of validation.

11. Describe and give an example of each of these types of validity checks: alphabetic, numeric, range, consistency, completeness, and check digit.

12. Explain how a file processing system works. Identify two weaknesses of a file processing system.

13. Explain how the database approach works. Identify five strengths of the database approach. Identify some disadvantages of the database approach.

14. Explain why a database cannot completely eliminate redundant data.

15. Identify the database vendors with the largest market share.

16. Identify the types of details stored in a data dictionary.

17. Define the term, query.

18. Describe the purpose of these file retrieval and maintenance tools: query language, query by example (QBE), form, and report generator.

19. Identify the purpose of a wizard.

20. Define access privileges. Explain the intent of the principle of least privilege.

21. Describe the purpose of backups, logs, recovery utilities, and continuous backup.

22. Define data model. Name examples.

23. A user of a relational database refers to a file as a(n) _____, a record as a(n) _____, and a field as a(n) _____.

24. A developer of a relational database refers to a file as a(n) _____, a record as a(n) _____, and a field as a(n) _____.

25. Describe the organization of relational databases. Define the term, relationship.

26. SQL stands for _____.

27. Differentiate between SQL and OQL.

28. Describe the organization of object-oriented databases.

29. Describe the organization of multidimensional databases.

30. Explain the purpose of data warehouses.

31. Give examples of databases on the Web.

32. Identify guidelines for designing a database.

33. Differentiate between a database analyst and a database administrator.

34. Identify ways computers and databases are used in the health sciences field.

35. Larry Ellison founded _____.

Check This Out

As technology changes, you must keep up with updates, new products, breakthroughs, and recent advances to remain digitally literate. The list below identifies topics related to this chapter that you should explore to keep current. In parentheses beside each topic, you will find a search term to help begin your research using a search engine, such as Google.

For current news and information
Check us out on Facebook and Twitter. See your instructor or the Computer Concepts CourseMate for specific information.

1. widely used databases in education (search for: popular databases education)

2. recent government dragnets used to fight crime (search for: latest government dragnets)

3. popular data validation techniques (search for: latest data validation checks)

4. updates about database management systems (search for: recent database management systems features)

5. largest database management systems market share (search for: top market share database management systems)

6. recent data security breaches (search for: security breaches news)

7. popular database backup and recovery techniques (search for: latest database backup recovery)

8. new relational database software (search for: relational database news)

9. popular business object-oriented databases (search for: objected-oriented database business)

10. recent uses of multidimensional databases (search for: multidimensional database examples)

11. new GIS databases available from the U.S. Geological Survey (search for: USGS Global GIS)

12. widely used Web databases (search for: popular Web databases)

13. updates about database administrator jobs (search for: database administrator duties)

14. developments of identifying species using DNA barcoding (search for: DNA barcoding news)

15. updates about Oracle's social network applications (search for: Oracle Public Cloud)

Computer Security and Safety, Ethics, and Privacy

Chapter 10

Why Should I Learn About Computer Security and Safety, Ethics, and Privacy?

"I am careful when browsing the Internet and never open e-mail messages from unknown senders. No one would guess that I use my dog's name as my password on home and school networks. I use a surge protector and an ENERGY STAR monitor. What more do I need to know about security, ethics, and privacy while using a computer or mobile device?"

True, you may be familiar with some of the material in this chapter, but do you know . . .

"What more do I need to know about security, ethics, and privacy while using a computer or mobile device?"

- How to tell if your computer is a zombie? (p. 387, FAQ)
- How to create a secure password? (p. 390, User Names and Passwords)
- How to prevent tendonitis, eye strain, and other injuries? (p. 398, Computers and Health Risks)
- Which merchants analyze your conversations and shopping habits? (p. 402, Innovative Computing)
- How computers monitor and maintain national and local security? (p. 408, Computer Usage @ Work)
- Who is one of the world's leading computer security experts? (p. 409, Technology Trailblazers)
- How to back up files on an offsite Internet server? (p. 414 and Computer Concepts CourseMate, Learn How To)
- How to receive system updates automatically? (Windows Exercises, Computer Concepts CourseMate)

For these answers and to discover much more information essential to this course, read Chapter 10 and visit the associated Computer Concepts CourseMate at www.cengagebrain.com.

Customize Your Learning Experience

Q & A | How can I meet one or more of these goals?

Make use of the goal's resources for each chapter in the book and you should meet that goal by the end of the course.

Adapt this book to meet your needs by determining your goal. Would you like to be an informed digital consumer? A productive technology user? A safe user, protected from the risks in a digital world? A competent digital citizen? A future entrepreneur or professional in a digital society?

Every chapter in this Student Success Guide identifies resources targeted toward each of these goals, along with criteria to verify you understand the resources' content. Resources may be located in the textbook, on the Computer Concepts CourseMate Web site, in the interactive eBook, and on the Web.

Informed Digital Consumer

Goal: I would like to understand the terminology used in Web or print advertisements that sell computers, mobile devices, and related technology, as well as the jargon used by sales associates in computer or electronics stores, so that I can make informed purchasing decisions.

Topic	Resource	Location	Now you should . . .
McAfee	Text	p. 409	Be familiar with McAfee's products and services
	Link	eBook p. 409 or CourseMate	
Symantec	Text	p. 409	Be familiar with Symantec's products and services
	Link	eBook p. 409 or CourseMate	

Productive Technology User

Goal: I would like to learn ways that technology can benefit me at home, work, and school. I also would like to learn helpful techniques for using technology so that I can perform tasks more efficiently and be more productive in daily activities.

Topic	Resource	Location	Now you should . . .
License Agreement	Text/Figure	p. 394	Know what is allowed and not allowed with a software license
Computer Ethics	Text/Figure	p. 400	Be aware of ethical/unethical computer uses
	Labs	CourseMate	
Cookies	Text/Figure	pp. 403–404	Know the uses of cookies, how they work, and how to view accepted cookies, and adjust cookie settings
	Web Link	eBook p. 404 or CourseMate	
	Labs	CourseMate	
Privacy Laws	Text/Figure	pp. 406–407	Be familiar with the intent of various privacy laws
	Drag and Drop Figure 10-25	eBook p. 406 or CourseMate	
Windows Media Player	Windows Exercises	CourseMate	Know how to use Windows Media Player to play a CD
Windows Updates	Windows Exercises	CourseMate	Know how to use Windows Update
Offsite Backup	Learn How To	pp. 414–415 and CourseMate	Know how to back up files to an offsite Internet server
Dictionary	Web Apps	CourseMate	Know how to use Dictionary.com

Safe User, Protected from the Risks in a Digital World

Goal: I would like to take measures to (1) protect my computers, devices, and data from loss, damage, or misuse; (2) minimize or prevent risks associated with using technology; and (3) minimize the environmental impact of using computers and related devices.

Topic	Resource	Location	Now you should . . .
Viruses and Other Malware	Text/Figures	pp. 385–387	Know ways to protect computers and devices from viruses and other malware
	Videos	eBook p. 387 or CourseMate	
		At the Movies, CourseMate	
Botnets	FAQ Link and Video	eBook p. 387, or Zombies and Botnets link, CourseMate	Know how to protect a computer from botnets
Firewalls	Text/Figure	pp. 388–389	Know how firewalls protect network resources
Unauthorized Access	Text	p. 389	Know how to protect your computer from unauthorized intrusions
Passwords	Text/Figure	pp. 390–391	Know how to select a good password
PINs	Text	p. 391	Know the uses of PINs and why you should select them carefully
Identity Theft	FAQ Link	eBook p. 392, or Identity Theft link, CourseMate	Know ways to protect yourself from identity theft
Hardware Theft	Text/Figure	p. 393	Be aware of ways to protect against hardware theft
Surge Protectors	Text/Figures	p. 396	Know the purpose of surge protectors and how they work
	Web Link	eBook p. 396 or CourseMate	

Continued on next page

Continued from previous page

Topic	Resource	Location	Now you should . . .
Wireless Security	Text	p. 397	Be familiar with ways to improve the security of wireless networks
Health Risks	Text/Figures	pp. 398–400	Know how to protect yourself from RSIs and CVS, how to design an ergonomic work area, and recognize computer addiction
Information Accuracy	Text	p. 400	Recognize that not all information is accurate
Green Computing	Text/Figure	pp. 401–402	Know strategies that support green computing
Information Privacy	Text/Figure	pp. 402–403	Know ways to safeguard personal information
Consumer Privacy	Innovative Computing	p. 402	Be aware that your shopping behaviors may be recorded and tracked to create consumer profiles
	Link	eBook p. 402 or CourseMate	
Electronic Profiles	Text/Figure	p. 403	Be aware how direct marketers create electronic profiles
Spyware and Adware	Text	p. 404	Know how to remove spyware and adware
Spam	Text/Figure	pp. 404–405	Know how to reduce amount of spam received
Phishing	Text/Figure	p. 405	Know how to protect yourself from phishing and pharming scams
Social Engineering	Text	p. 405	Be familiar with social engineering scams
Content Filtering	Text/Figure	p. 407	Be familiar with issues surrounding content filtering and Web filtering

Competent Digital Citizen

Goal: I would like to be knowledgeable and well-informed about computers, mobile devices, and related technology, so that I am digitally literate in my personal and professional use of digital devices.

Topic	Resource	Location	Now you should . . .
Security Risks	Text	p. 382	Know the definition of computer security risks
Cybercrime	Text	pp. 382–383	Be familiar with the categories of cybercriminals
Malware	Text/Figure and FAQ	pp. 384–385	Know the types of malware, how infections spread, and common symptoms of their infection
	FAQ Link	eBook p. 385, or Infected Media Files link, CourseMate	
Botnets, DoS Attacks, Back Doors, Spoofing	Text and FAQ	pp. 387–388	Know the intent of botnets, DoS attacks, back doors, and spoofing
	Web Link	eBook p. 387 or CourseMate	
CAPTCHAs	Text	p. 390	Know the purpose of CAPTCHAs
Brain Fingerprinting	Looking Ahead	p. 392	Know how brain fingerprints and behavior detection systems could be used in crime scene investigations
	Link and Video	eBook p. 392 or CourseMate	
Software Theft	Text	p. 393	Be familiar with types of software theft
Encryption	Text/Figures	pp. 395–396	Know how encryption works
	Drag and Drop Figure 10-11	eBook p. 395 or CourseMate	
	Animation		

Continued on next page

Continued from previous page

Topic	Resource	Location	Now you should . . .
Electrical Power Variations	Text	p. 396	Know the impact of electrical power variations
War Driving	Text/Figure	p. 397	Be able to describe war driving
IP Rights	Text	p. 401	Be aware of intellectual property rights
Richard Stallman	Text	p. 409	Be familiar with Richard Stallman's copyleft concept
	Link and Video	eBook p. 409 or CourseMate	
Gene Spafford	Text	p. 409	Be familiar with Gene Spafford's role in computer security
	Link	eBook p. 409 or CourseMate	

Future Entrepreneur or Professional in a Digital Society

Goal: As I ponder my future, I envision myself as an entrepreneur or skilled professional using technology to support my business endeavors or job responsibilities. Along the way, I may interact with a variety of computer professionals — or I may just become one myself!

Topic	Resource	Location	Now you should . . .
Firewalls	Text	pp. 388–389	Be familiar with how enterprises use hardware firewalls
	Video	eBook p. 389 or CourseMate	
Intrusion Detection	Text	p. 389	Know why organizations use intrusion detection software
Authenticating Users	Text/Figures	pp. 389–391	Know how organizations identify and authenticate users through user names, passwords, possessed objects, and biometrics
Digital Forensics	Text	p. 392	Know the purpose and uses of digital forensics
RTLS	Text	p. 393	Know the purpose and uses of real time location systems
	Web Link	eBook p. 393 or CourseMate	
Digital Signatures and Certificates	Text/Figures	pp. 395–396	Know why organizations use digital signatures and digital certificates
UPS	Text/Figure	p. 396	Know how organizations use UPS devices
Backing Up	Text	pp. 396–397	Know the types of backups used by organizations
Employee Monitoring	Text Ethics & Issues	p. 407	Know issues surrounding employers monitoring employee communications
National and Local Security	Computer Usage @ Work	p. 408	Know how governments and businesses have implemented new security measures
	Link and Video	eBook p. 408 or CourseMate	
Digital Forensics Examiner	Exploring Computer Careers	CourseMate	Be familiar with the responsibilities and education required for digital forensics examiners

Preparing for a Test

Visit the Computer Concepts CourseMate at www.cengagebrain.com and then navigate to the Chapter 10 Web Apps resource for this book to prepare for your test.

Does your class use the Computer Concepts CourseMate Web site? If so, prepare for your test by using the Flash Cards, Study Guide, and Practice Test Web apps — available for your smart phone or tablet.

If your class does not use the Computer Concepts CourseMate Web site or you prefer to use your book, you can prepare for the test by doing the Quiz Yourself activities on pages 392, 397, and 408; reading the Chapter Review on pages 410–411; ensuring you know the definitions for the terms on page 411; and completing the Checkpoint exercises on page 412. You also should know the material identified in the Chapter 10 Study Guide that follows.

Chapter 10 Study Guide

This study guide identifies material you should know for the Chapter 10 exam. You may want to write the answers in a notebook, enter them on your digital device, record them into a phone, or highlight them in your book. Choose whichever method helps you remember the best.

1. Define the term, computer security risk.
2. Define the terms, computer crime and cybercrime.
3. Differentiate among a hacker, cracker, script kiddie, corporate spy, unethical employee, cyberextortionist, and cyberterrorist.
4. Differentiate among a computer virus, worm, Trojan horse, and rootkit.
5. Malware is short for _____.
6. Define the term, payload. Identify various ways a payload is delivered.
7. Identify ways to safeguard against computer viruses and other malware.
8. Describe the purpose of an antivirus program. Explain techniques used by antivirus programs.
9. Define the terms, botnet and zombie. Describe ways to tell if a computer is a zombie or in a botnet.
10. DoS stands for _____. Explain how a DoS attack works. Identify reasons perpetrators claim to carry out a DoS attack.
11. Explain how a back door works.
12. Describe spoofing.
13. Define the term, firewall. Identify uses of firewalls.
14. Describe the purpose of intrusion detection software.
15. AUP stands for _____.
16. Describe an access control.
17. Define the terms, user name and password.
18. Explain the purpose and use of CAPTCHAs.
19. Give examples of possessed objects that might use a PIN.
20. Identify the purpose of biometric devices.
21. Define digital forensics. Describe requirements of a digital forensics examiner.
22. Identify safeguards against hardware theft and vandalism.
23. Define software piracy. Explain the ways software manufacturers protect against software piracy.
24. Define a license agreement. Identify actions that are allowed and not allowed according to a license agreement.
25. Discuss the encryption process.
26. Describe the purpose of digital signatures and digital certificates.
27. Identify causes of system failure.
28. Discuss surge protectors and UPSs.
29. Explain the options available for backing up computer resources.
30. Describe the purpose of war driving. Identify ways to secure a wireless network.
31. RSI stands for _____. Identify two types of RSIs and precautions to prevent these injuries.
32. Describe symptoms of computer vision syndrome. Identify techniques to ease eyestrain.
33. Define ergonomics. Give examples of an ergonomically designed work area.
34. Identify symptoms of computer addiction.
35. Explain why users cannot assume information always is correct.
36. Describe intellectual property rights. Explain issues related to copyright law.
37. Describe green computing strategies.
38. Identify ways to safeguard personal information.
39. Explain how electronic profiles are created.
40. Define cookie. Identify uses of cookies.

Continued on next page

Continued from previous page

41. Describe spyware, adware, and spam. Explain ways to remove spyware and adware, and to reduce spam.

42. Define phishing. Identify ways to protect yourself from phishing scams.

43. Define social engineering.

44. Identify common points in laws surrounding privacy.

45. Discuss issues surrounding employee monitoring and content filtering.

46. Name two companies that sell products that protect computers and devices from malware, spam, and unauthorized access.

Check This Out

As technology changes, you must keep up with updates, new products, breakthroughs, and recent advances to remain digitally literate. The list below identifies topics related to this chapter that you should explore to keep current. In parentheses beside each topic, you will find a search term to help begin your research using a search engine, such as Google.

For current news and information
Check us out on Facebook and Twitter. See your instructor or the Computer Concepts CourseMate for specific information.

1. **recent attempts to stop cybercrime activities** (search for: fighting cybercrime)

2. **latest CERT/CC security breach notices** (search for: CERT announcements)

3. **popular malware block and removal tools** (search for: top malware removal software)

4. **news of denial of service attacks** (search for: recent DoS DDoS attacks)

5. **popular antivirus programs** (search for: top antivirus programs)

6. **new biometric identification devices** (search for: biometric device systems)

7. **recent real time location system applications** (search for: latest RTLS)

8. **new products to curb hardware theft and vandalism** (search for: computer hardware theft deterrent)

9. **current Business Software Alliance efforts to fight software piracy** (search for: BSA piracy news)

10. **current encryption software** (search for: new encryption technology)

11. **new surge protectors and uninterruptible power supplies** (search for: popular surge protectors UPS)

12. **latest home wireless security network trends** (search for: home wireless network security software)

13. **updates about computer addiction treatments** (search for: computer addiction therapy)

14. **current green computing initiatives** (search for: green computing concepts)

15. **recent phishing and smishing scams** (search for: phishing smishing attacks)

Information System Development and Programming Languages

Chapter 11

Why Should I Learn About Information System Development and Programming Languages?

"My school is updating its computer system. The conversion process has been lengthy, but some new features are useful. When my boss needs to update his payroll program, he hires a programmer to make changes. Although these modifications are interesting, why do I need to learn more about computer system development and programming languages?"

True, you may be familiar with some of the material in this chapter, but do you know . . .

"Why do I need to learn more about computer system development and programming languages?"

- Who is involved in developing a new information system? (p. 419, Who Participates in System Development?)
- Where organizations are likely to locate value-added resellers? (p. 429, FAQ)
- How you can view billions of remote galaxy images on your computer? (p. 431, Looking Ahead)
- How Web Page authoring software is used to create Web pages? (p. 449, Web Page Authoring Software)
- How automakers use computers to streamline manufacturing? (p. 454, Computer Usage @ Work)
- Which software company develops the FIFA, Madden NFL, and Need for Speed Undercover video games? (p. 455, Companies on the Cutting Edge)
- How to gather information in a personal interview? (p. 460 and Computer Concepts CourseMate, Learn How To)
- How to adjust the speed of your keyboard? (Windows Exercises, Computer Concepts CourseMate)

For these answers and to discover much more information essential to this course, read Chapter 11 and visit the associated Computer Concepts CourseMate at www.cengagebrain.com.

Customize Your Learning Experience

Q & A How can I meet one or more of these goals?

Make use of the goal's resources for each chapter in the book and you should meet that goal by the end of the course.

Adapt this book to meet your needs by determining your goal. Would you like to be an informed digital consumer? A productive technology user? A safe user, protected from the risks in a digital world? A competent digital citizen? A future entrepreneur or professional in a digital society?

Every chapter in this Student Success Guide identifies resources targeted toward each of these goals, along with criteria to verify you understand the resources' content. Resources may be located in the textbook, on the Computer Concepts CourseMate Web site, in the interactive eBook, and on the Web.

Informed Digital Consumer

Goal: I would like to understand the terminology used in Web or print advertisements that sell computers, mobile devices, and related technology, as well as the jargon used by sales associates in computer or electronics stores, so that I can make informed purchasing decisions.

Topic	Resource	Location	Now you should . . .
Project Management	Text	p. 420	Know the purpose of project management software
EA	Text	p. 455	Be familiar with entertainment products by Electronic Arts
	Link	eBook p. 455 or CourseMate	
	Video	At the Movies, CourseMate	

Productive Technology User

Goal: I would like to learn ways that technology can benefit me at home, work, and school. I also would like to learn helpful techniques for using technology so that I can perform tasks more efficiently and be more productive in daily activities.

Topic	Resource	Location	Now you should . . .
Interviews	Learn How To	pp. 460–461	Know how to conduct various types of interviews and questions to expect as an interviewee
Project Request	Text	p. 423	Know how to initiate a system development project
E-Zine	Text	p. 428	Be familiar with an e-zine and name popular ones
	Web Link	eBook p. 428 or CourseMate	
Prototype	Text	p. 431	Know the purpose of a prototype
Online Calculators	Innovative Computing	p. 439	Know popular calculators on the Web
	Link	eBook p. 439 or CourseMate	
4GLs	Text and FAQ	p. 443	Be familiar with the purpose of 4GLs and SQL
	FAQ Link	eBook p. 443 or CourseMate	
Application Generator	Text/Figure	pp. 444–445	Be familiar with the use of application generators
Macros	Text	p. 445	Know the purpose of macros and how to create them
	Web Link	eBook p. 445 or CourseMate	
Program Files, Loans, and Keyboard Speed	Windows Exercises	CourseMate	Know how to search for executable files, use the Loan Payment Calculator Program, and adjust keyboard speed
Google Earth	Web Apps	CourseMate	Know how to use Google Earth to view locations and images

Safe User, Protected from the Risks in a Digital World

Goal: I would like to take measures to (1) protect my computers, devices, and data from loss, damage, or misuse; (2) minimize or prevent risks associated with using technology; and (3) minimize the environmental impact of using computers and related devices.

Topic	Resource	Location	Now you should . . .
Financial Web Sites	FAQ	p. 435	Be aware of vulnerabilities associated with financial Web sites
Macro Security	Ethics & Issues	p. 445	Be aware of security threats surrounding macros
Computer Security	Text	p. 434	Be familiar with the purpose of a computer security plan

Competent Digital Citizen

Goal: I would like to be knowledgeable and well-informed about computers, mobile devices, and related technology, so that I am digitally literate in my personal and professional use of digital devices.

Topic	Resource	Location	Now you should . . .
SDLC	Text/Figure	p. 418	Be able to identify the phases in an SDLC
Documentation	Text	p. 422	Know the types of documentation in system development
Data and Information Gathering	Text/Figure/FAQ	pp. 422–423	Know the purpose of reviewing documentation, observing, surveying, interviewing, conducting JAD sessions, and researching; be able to explain the Hawthorne Effect
	Ethics & Issues		
	Video	eBook p. 422 or CourseMate	

Continued on next page

64 Student Success Guide

Continued from previous page

Topic	Resource	Location	Now you should . . .
Packaged vs. Custom Software	Text	p. 427	Know the difference between packaged and custom software, and the difference between horizontal and vertical market software
	Web Link	eBook p. 427 or CourseMate	
LSST	Looking Ahead	p. 431	Know how the Large Synoptic Survey Telescope will provide a graphical view of the universe's evolution
	Link and Video	eBook p. 431 or CourseMate	
CASE Tools	Text/Figure	p. 432	Know the purpose and use of CASE tools
Conversion Strategies	Text	pp. 433–434	Know differences among direct, parallel, phased, and pilot conversions
Web App Vulnerabilities	FAQ Link	eBook p. 435 or CourseMate	Know how to test a Web application's vulnerabilities
Programming Lang.	Text/Figure	pp. 435–436	Be able to describe programming languages
Low- vs. High-Level	Text	p. 436	Know the difference between low-level and high-level languages
Machine Language	Text/Figure	p. 436	Know the purpose of machine language
Assembly Language	Text/Figure	p. 437	Know the purpose of an assembly language
Source Program	Text	p. 437	Be able to define source program
Procedural Languages	Text	p. 438	Describe procedural languages
Compilers vs. Interpreters	Text/Figures	pp. 438–439	Be able to differentiate between compilers and interpreters
C and COBOL	Text/Figures	pp. 439–440	Know the uses of C and COBOL
OOP Languages/Tools	Text/Figures	p. 440	Describe object-oriented programming languages, RAD, and IDE
Java, .NET, C++, C#, F#, Delphi, PowerBuilder	Text/Figure	pp. 440–443	Know the characteristics and uses of Java, .NET, C++, C#, F#, Delphi, and PowerBuilder
	Web Link	eBook p. 441 or CourseMate	
Visual Studio	Text/Figure	pp. 441–443	Know the purpose of and languages in the Visual Studio suite, visual programming, and user interface design
	Labs	CourseMate	
Classic Programming Languages	Text/Figure	p. 444	Know the purpose of several classic programming languages
HTML, XHTML, XML, and WML	Text/Figure	pp. 446–447	Know the characteristics and uses of HTML, XHTML, XML, and WML
	Link and Video	eBook p. 447 or CourseMate	
Scripts, Applets, Servlets, and ActiveX	Text	p. 447	Know the differences among scripts, applets, servlets, and ActiveX controls
Scripting Languages	Text/Figure	pp. 447–448	Know the purpose of JavaScript, Perl, PHP, Rexx, Tcl, and VBScript
	Web Link	eBook p. 448 or CourseMate	
DHTML, Ruby on Rails	Text	p. 448	Know the uses of DHTML and the purpose of Ruby on Rails
Web 2.0 Development	Text/Figure	p. 448	Be familiar with tools used to develop Web 2.0 sites and APIs
Web Page Authoring	Text	p. 449	Know about Dreamweaver, Expression Web, Flash, and SharePoint Designer
Multimedia Develop.	Text/Figure	p. 449	Be familiar with the purpose of multimedia authoring software
Program Development	Text/Figures	pp. 450–451	Know the steps in the program development life cycle and how it relates to the SDLC
Control Structures	Text/Figures	pp. 451–453	Know the differences among sequence, selection, and repetition control structures
	Figure 11-33 Animation	eBook p. 453 or CourseMate	

Continued on next page

Continued from previous page

Topic	Resource	Location	Now you should . . .
Ed Yourdon	Text	p. 455	Be familiar with Ed Yourdon's contributions to computer technology
	Link	eBook p. 455 or CourseMate	
James Gosling	Text	p. 455	Be familiar with James Gosling's contributions to the computer field
	Link and Video	eBook p. 455 or CourseMate	

Future Entrepreneur or Professional in a Digital Society

Goal: As I ponder my future, I envision myself as an entrepreneur or skilled professional using technology to support my business endeavors or job responsibilities. Along the way, I may interact with a variety of computer professionals — or I may just become one myself!

Topic	Resource	Location	Now you should . . .
System Development	Text/Figure	pp. 418–419	Be able to describe an information system and system development, and know system development guidelines
System Development Participants	Text/Figure	pp. 419–420	Know the role of analysts, users, the steering committees, and others during system development
	Drag and Drop Figure 11-2	eBook p. 419 or CourseMate	
Project Management	Text/Figure	pp. 420–421	Know how organizations use project management and the difference between Gantt and PERT charts
	Links and Video	eBook pp. 420–421 or CourseMate	
	Labs	CourseMate	
Feasibility	Text	p. 421	Know the tests organizations use to assess project feasibility
Systems Analyst	FAQ	p. 422	Know the role of, responsibilities of, and education required for a systems analyst
	FAQ Link	eBook p. 422 or CourseMate	
Planning Phase	Text	p. 425	Know the major activities performed in the planning phase
Analysis Phase	Text	p. 425	Know the major activities performed in the analysis phase
Preliminary Investigation	Text/Figure	pp. 425–426	Know the purpose of the preliminary investigation and contents of the feasibility report
Detailed Analysis	Text	p. 427	Know the major activities performed during detailed analysis
System Proposal	Text	p. 427	Know the purpose of the system proposal
Outsourcing	Text	p. 428	Be familiar with outsourcing
Design Phase	Text/Figure	p. 428	Know the major activities performed in the design phase
RFQ, RFP, RFI, VAR	Text and FAQ	pp. 428–429	Know the difference of an RFQ, RFP, and RFI, and the purpose of a VAR
IT Consultants	Text	p. 429	Know the role of IT consultants
Detailed Design	Text/Figures	pp. 430–431	Know the major activities performed during detailed design
Quality Review	Text	p. 432	Be familiar with who participates in a quality review
Implementation Phase	Text/Figure	pp. 432–433	Know the major activities performed during the implementation phase
Operation, Support, and Security Phase	Text	pp. 434–435	Know the major activities performed during the operation, support, and security phase
Chief Security Officer	Text	p. 434	Know the role and responsibilities of a chief security officer

Continued on next page

Continued from previous page

Topic	Resource	Location	Now you should . . .
Programmer	Text	p. 435	Know the role and responsibilities of and the education required for a computer programmer
	Exploring Computer Careers	CourseMate	
Popular Web Programming Languages	FAQ	p. 449	Be familiar with popular Web programming languages
	FAQ Link	eBook p. 449 or CourseMate	
Programming Team	Text	p. 451	Know the purpose of a programming team
Computers in Manufacturing	Computer Usage @ Work	p. 454	Know how computers are used in the manufacture of cars
	Link and Video	eBook p. 454 or CourseMate	
CSC	Text	p. 455	Be familiar with services provided by Computer Sciences Corporation
	Link	eBook p. 455 or CourseMate	

Preparing for a Test

Visit the Computer Concepts CourseMate at www.cengagebrain.com and then navigate to the Chapter 11 Web Apps resource for this book to prepare for your test.

Does your class use the Computer Concepts CourseMate Web site? If so, prepare for your test by using the Flash Cards, Study Guide, and Practice Test Web apps — available for your smart phone or tablet.

If your class does not use the Computer Concepts CourseMate Web site or you prefer to use your book, you can prepare for the test by doing the Quiz Yourself activities on pages 435, 450, and 454; reading the Chapter Review on pages 456–457; ensuring you know the definitions for the terms on page 457; and completing the Checkpoint exercises on page 458. You also should know the material identified in the Chapter 11 Study Guide that follows.

Chapter 11 Study Guide

This study guide identifies material you should know for the Chapter 11 exam. You may want to write the answers in a notebook, enter them on your digital device, record them into a phone, or highlight them in your book. Choose whichever method helps you remember the best.

1. Describe an information system. Define system development.

2. SDLC stands for _____. Name the five phases that often are part of an SDLC. Name and briefly describe the major activities performed in each of these phases.

3. Describe the three guidelines that system development should follow.

4. Describe the role of a systems analyst.

5. Define the purpose of a steering committee. Identify the composition of a project team.

6. Explain project management. Differentiate between a Gantt chart and a PERT chart. Describe the purpose of change management.

7. Define feasibility. Differentiate among operational, schedule, technical, and economic feasibility.

8. Describe data and information gathering techniques: review documentation, observe, survey, interview, conduct JAD sessions, and research.

9. Explain the Hawthorne Effect.

10. Explain the purpose of a project request and a feasibility study.

11. Name the activities performed during detailed analysis.

12. Identify the purpose of the system proposal.

13. Differentiate between packaged software and custom software. Describe outsourcing. Differentiate between horizontal and vertical market software.

14. Name the major tasks performed when acquiring hardware and software.

15. RFQ stands for _____. RFP stands for _____. RFI stands for _____. Differentiate among these three documents.

16. Describe the function of a VAR (value-added reseller).

17. Describe an IT consultant.

18. Described the activities performed during detailed design.

19. Describe the purpose of a prototype and CASE tools.

20. Differentiate among a unit test, systems test, integration test, and acceptance test.

21. Describe various training methods.

Continued on next page

Continued from previous page

22. Differentiate among direct conversion, parallel conversion, phased conversion, and pilot conversion.

23. Identify the role of a CSO (chief security officer). Identify the purpose of a computer security plan.

24. Define computer program and programming language. Another term for programmer is _____.

25. Differentiate between low-level and high-level languages.

26. Define machine language.

27. Describe how a programmer writes assembly language instructions and the purpose of an assembler.

28. Define source program.

29. Describe how a programmer writes procedural language instructions.

30. Differentiate between a compiler and an interpreter.

31. Identify uses of C and COBOL.

32. Define an object. Describe advantages of object-oriented programming languages.

33. RAD stands for _____. Describe RAD.

34. Name the company that developed Java.

35. Describe the purpose of the .NET Framework.

36. Briefly discuss characteristics of C++, C#, and F#, Delphi, and PowerBuilder.

37. Describe Visual Studio. Differentiate among Visual Basic, Visual C++, and Visual C#.

38. Define visual programming language.

39. Describe how a programmer writes nonprocedural language instructions. Name a popular 4GL.

40. Describe the purpose of application generators.

41. Define macro. Describe two techniques for creating macros.

42. Describe the purpose of HTML, XHTML, XML, WML, RSS 2.0, and ATOM.

43. Discuss and identify uses of scripts, applets, servlets, and ActiveX controls.

44. Differentiate among JavaScript, Perl, PHP, Rexx, Tcl, and VBScript.

45. Identify the purpose of DHTML, Ruby on Rails, and Ajax.

46. API stands for _____.

47. Describe the purpose of Web page authoring software and multimedia authoring software. Name some examples.

48. PDLC stands for _____. Name the six steps in the PDLC. Differentiate between sequence, selection, and repetition control structures.

49. Identify the type of software developed by Electronic Arts.

Check This Out

As technology changes, you must keep up with updates, new products, breakthroughs, and recent advances to remain digitally literate. The list below identifies topics related to this chapter that you should explore to keep current. In parentheses beside each topic, you will find a search term to help begin your research using a search engine, such as Google.

For current news and information
Check us out on Facebook and Twitter. See your instructor or the Computer Concepts CourseMate for specific information.

1. **latest information system developments** (search for: information system news)

2. **popular project management software** (search for: top project management software)

3. **news on SDLC trends** (search for: SDLC planning)

4. **latest outsourcing statistics** (search for: outsourcing trends)

5. **popular value-added resellers** (search for: top value-added software hardware resellers)

6. **widely used conversion strategies** (search for: conversion strategies)

7. **widely used programming languages** (search for: popular programming languages)

8. **high-level programming languages to know** (search for: best high-level programming learn)

9. **current uses of assembly languages** (search for: assembly code example)

10. **popular rapid application development components** (search for: top RAD environment tools)

11. **new Microsoft Visual Studio tools** (search for: Visual Studio features)

12. **new fourth-generation languages** (search for: latest fourth-generation programming languages)

13. **popular RSS and ATOM XML applications** (search for: XML applications RSS ATOM)

14. **popular Web programming languages** (search for: top Web programming languages)

15. **widely used Web page authoring software** (search for: popular Web page authoring programs)

Student Success Guide

Enterprise Computing

Why Should I Learn About Enterprise Computing?

"My neighbor owns a small manufacturing business, and I often assist him on weekends by billing his customers and updating his budget. I back up the data on his computer to a USB flash drive and plan to expand his business interactions over the Internet. These computer functions seem adequate, so why should I learn about enterprise computing?"

True, you may be familiar with some of the material in this chapter, but do you know . . .

"Why should I learn about enterprise computing?"

- How various units function within a business? (p. 468, Information Systems in the Enterprise)
- Why data may be stored in the tundra and in abandoned coal mines? (p. 479, Innovative Computing)
- Why practically everyone soon may be using cloud computing? (p. 483, Cloud and Grid Computing)
- What hardware you can use to back up data on your computer continuously? (p. 491, FAQ)
- How municipalities use computers to enhance services? (p. 492, Computer Usage @ Work)
- Which YouTube cofounder created PayPal's original logo? (p. 493, Companies on the Cutting Edge)
- How to use Skype to make unlimited calls? (p. 498 and Computer Concepts CourseMate, Learn How To)
- How to create a desktop shortcut to print? (Windows Exercises, Computer Concepts CourseMate)

For these answers and to discover much more information essential to this course, read Chapter 12 and visit the associated Computer Concepts CourseMate at www.cengagebrain.com.

Q & A

How can I meet one or more of these goals?

Make use of the goal's resources for each chapter in the book and you should meet that goal by the end of the course.

Customize Your Learning Experience

Adapt this book to meet your needs by determining your goal. Would you like to be an informed digital consumer? A productive technology user? A safe user, protected from the risks in a digital world? A competent digital citizen? A future entrepreneur or professional in a digital society?

Every chapter in this Student Success Guide identifies resources targeted toward each of these goals, along with criteria to verify you understand the resources' content. Resources may be located in the textbook, on the Computer Concepts CourseMate Web site, in the interactive eBook, and on the Web.

Informed Digital Consumer

Goal: I would like to understand the terminology used in Web or print advertisements that sell computers, mobile devices, and related technology, as well as the jargon used by sales associates in computer or electronics stores, so that I can make informed purchasing decisions.

Topic	Resource	Location	Now you should . . .
Living Digitally	Text/Figures	pp. 501–506	Be familiar with audio, video, recording, gaming, and digital home products you may find useful

Productive Technology User

Goal: I would like to learn ways that technology can benefit me at home, work, and school. I also would like to learn helpful techniques for using technology so that I can perform tasks more efficiently and be more productive in daily activities.

Topic	Resource	Location	Now you should . . .
E-Commerce	Text/Figure	pp. 484–485	Know the online services that users find beneficial: e-retail, finance, travel, entertainment and media, and health
	Drag and Drop Figure 12-20	eBook p. 484 or CourseMate	
Computers in Municipal Services	Computer Usage @ Work	p. 492	Know how you interact with or benefit from computers in various municipal services
	Link and Video	eBook p. 492 or CourseMate	
VoIP	Learn How To	pp. 498–499 and CourseMate	Know how to use VoIP (Voice over Internet Protocol)
Changing Windows Views	Windows Exercises	CourseMate	Know how to change views in Windows
Desktop Shortcuts	Windows Exercises	CourseMate	Know how to create a desktop shortcut in Windows
Sounds Cards and Audio Devices	Windows Exercises	CourseMate	Know how to determine the brand and model of sound cards and audio devices on your computer
Microsoft Office Web Apps	Web Apps	CourseMate	Know how to use Microsoft Office Web Apps to create, edit, and share documents, workbooks, presentations, and notes

Safe User, Protected from the Risks in a Digital World

Goal: I would like to take measures to (1) protect my computers, devices, and data from loss, damage, or misuse; (2) minimize or prevent risks associated with using technology; and (3) minimize the environmental impact of using computers and related devices.

Topic	Resource	Location	Now you should . . .
Personal Information	FAQ	p. 473	Know to be careful when supplying personal information to companies
	FAQ Link	eBook p. 473, or Sharing Personal Information link, CourseMate	
Online Purchases	Ethics & Issues	p. 485	Be familiar with ways to safeguard online purchases
Backup Procedures	Text and FAQ	pp. 490–491	Know the difference in various backup methods: full, differential, incremental, selective, and continuous
Disaster Recovery Plan	Text	p. 491	Know the components of a disaster recovery plan
	Link and Video	eBook p. 491 or CourseMate	

Competent Digital Citizen

Goal: I would like to be knowledgeable and well-informed about computers, mobile devices, and related technology, so that I am digitally literate in my personal and professional use of digital devices.

Topic	Resource	Location	Now you should . . .
Portals	Text/Figure	pp. 479–480	Know the purpose and use of a portal
Data Warehouses	Text/Figure	pp. 480–481	Know the purpose and use of data warehouses
Extranets	Text	p. 481	Know the benefits of an extranet
Web Services	Text/Figure	pp. 481–482	Know how Web services work
	Drag and Drop Figure 12-18	eBook p. 482 or CourseMate	
	Web Link		
Workflow	Text	p. 482	Be familiar with workflow and workflow applications
VPN	Text/Figure	pp. 482–483	Know the purpose of a virtual private network
Virtualization	Text	p. 483	Be familiar with the benefits of and various types of virtualization
	Web Link	eBook p. 483 or CourseMate	
Cloud Computing	Text	pp. 483–484	Be familiar with trends in cloud computing
	Looking Ahead	p. 484	
	Video	eBook p. 484 or CourseMate	
Grid Computing	Text	p. 484	Know the purpose of grid computing
RAID	Text/Figure	p. 486	Know how RAID works
	Figure 12-21 Animation	eBook p. 486 or CourseMate	
NAS and SAN	Text/Figure	pp. 486–487	Know the purpose of network attached storage and storage area networks
	Web Link	eBook p. 486 or CourseMate	
Blade Servers	Text/Figure	p. 489	Know the purpose and advantages of blade servers
High-Availability Systems	Text/Figure	pp. 489–490	Be familiar with the uses of high-availability systems and the purpose of redundant components
Scalability	Text	p. 490	Know the definition of scalability
Interoperability	Text	p. 490	Know the definition of interoperability
EMC	Text	p. 493	Be familiar with EMC's products and services
	Link	eBook p. 493 or CourseMate	
IBM	Text	p. 493	Be familiar with IBM's products and services
	Link	eBook p. 493 or CourseMate	
Chad Hurley	Text	p. 493	Be familiar with Chad Hurley's contributions to technology
	Link and Video	eBook p. 493 or CourseMate	
Anita Borg	Text	p. 493	Be familiar with Anita Borg's role with women in technology
	Link	eBook p. 493 or CourseMate	

Goal: As I ponder my future, I envision myself as an entrepreneur or skilled professional using technology to support my business endeavors or job responsibilities. Along the way, I may interact with a variety of computer professionals — or I may just become one myself!

Topic	Resource	Location	Now you should . . .
Enterprise Computing	Text/Figure	pp. 464–465	Know the meaning of enterprise computing
Enterprise Types	Text	p. 466	Be familiar with various types of enterprises
Organizational Structure	Text/Figure	pp. 466–467	Be familiar with hierarchical structure of an organization
Levels of Users	Text/Figure	p. 467	Know the difference between decision levels and job titles for executive management, middle management, operational management, and nonmanagement employees
	Drag and Drop Figure 12-3	eBook p. 467 or CourseMate	
Management	Text	p. 468	Know how managers plan, organize, lead, and control; know how they use business intelligence, business process management, and business process automation
	Web Link	eBook p. 468 or CourseMate	
Functional Units	Text/Figures	pp. 468–473	Know the role of functional units in most organizations: accounting and finance, human resources, engineering, manufacturing, quality control, marketing, sales, distribution, customer service, and information technology
	Drag and Drop Figure 12-5	eBook p. 469 or CourseMate	
General Information Systems	Text/Figures	pp. 473–477	Be able to describe each type of general information system: office information system (OIS), transaction processing system (TPS), management information system (MIS), decision support system (DSS), and expert system
Integrated Information Systems	Text/Figures	pp. 477–478	Be able to describe each type of integrated information system: enterprise resource planning (ERP), customer relationship management (CRM), and content management system (CMS)
	Web Link	eBook p. 478 or CourseMate	
Data Centers	Text	p. 479	Be aware of the purpose of a data center and be familiar with some examples
	Innovative Computing		
	Link and Video	eBook p. 479 or CourseMate	
	Web Link		
	Video	At the Movies, CourseMate	
Wikis	FAQ	p. 486	Know why enterprises use wikis
Enterprise Storage	Text/Figure	pp. 487–488	Be familiar with storage strategies used by enterprises
Sarbanes-Oxley Act	Ethics & Issues	p. 488	Be familiar with financial reporting requirements defined by the Sarbanes-Oxley Act
CIO	Exploring Computer Careers	CourseMate	Be familiar with the responsibilities of and education required for a chief information officer (CIO)

Preparing for a Test

Visit the Computer Concepts CourseMate at www.cengagebrain.com and then navigate to the Chapter 12 Web Apps resource for this book to prepare for your test.

Does your class use the Computer Concepts CourseMate Web site? If so, prepare for your test by using the Flash Cards, Study Guide, and Practice Test Web apps — available for your smart phone or tablet.

If your class does not use the Computer Concepts CourseMate Web site or you prefer to use your book, you can prepare for the test by doing the Quiz Yourself activities on pages 479, 485, and 492; reading the Chapter Review on pages 494–495; ensuring you know the definitions for the terms on page 495; and completing the Checkpoint exercises on page 496. You also should know the material identified in the Chapter 12 Study Guide that follows.

Chapter 12 Study Guide

This study guide identifies material you should know for the Chapter 12 exam. You may want to write the answers in a notebook, enter them on your digital device, record them into a phone, or highlight them in your book. Choose whichever method helps you remember the best.

1. Define enterprise computing.

2. Know the purpose of these types of enterprises: retail, manufacturing, service, wholesale, government, educational, and transportation.

3. Identify the types of decisions and sample job titles of executive management, middle management, operational management, and nonmanagement employees.

4. Describe how managers plan, organize, lead, and control.

5. Define business intelligence, business process management, and business process automation.

6. Describe the purpose of and software used by these business functional units: accounting and finance, human resources, engineering or product development, manufacturing, quality control, marketing, sales, distribution, customer service, and information technology.

7. ERM stands for _____.

8. MRP stands for _____. Describe MRP.

9. Describe these general information systems: office information system (OIS), transaction processing system (TPS), management information system (MIS), decision support system (DSS), and expert system.

10. Differentiate online transaction processing (OLTP) from online analytical processing (OLAP).

11. Define the purpose of an executive information system (EIS).

12. AI stands for _____.

13. Describe AI.

14. Describe these integrated information systems: enterprise resource planning (ERP), customer relationship management (CRM), and content management systems (CMS).

15. Define data center.

16. Describe the purpose and capabilities of a portal.

17. Describe how data warehouses work.

18. Define click stream.

19. Identify uses of extranets.

20. Describe the purpose of Web services.

21. Describe a workflow and a workflow application.

22. Describe the purpose of a virtual private network (VPN).

23. Define virtualization. Give examples.

24. Identify benefits of cloud computing.

25. Define grid computing.

26. Explain the purpose of these e-commerce market segments: e-retail, finance, travel, entertainment and media, and health.

27. Identify ways to shop safely online.

28. Define legacy system.

29. Explain reasons enterprises use wikis.

30. Describe the purpose of RAID.

31. Describe the purpose of network attached storage and storage area networks.

32. Identify the goal of an enterprise storage system. Identify storage devices used by enterprise storage systems.

33. State the purpose of the Sarbanes-Oxley Act.

34. Describe a blade server.

35. Define high-availability system and redundant components.

36. Explain scalability and interoperability.

37. Differentiate among these backup methods: full, differential, incremental, selective, and continuous.

38. Describe the components of a disaster recovery plan.

39. Identify services provided by EMC.

40. _____ cofounded YouTube.

Check This Out

As technology changes, you must keep up with updates, new products, breakthroughs, and recent advances to remain digitally literate. The list below identifies topics related to this chapter that you should explore to keep current. In parentheses beside each topic, you will find a search term to help begin your research using a search engine, such as Google.

1. new enterprise organizational structure developments (search for: enterprise organization structure)

2. recent iPad and tablet computer uses in corporations (search for: iPad tablet corporations)

3. recent business process management developments (search for: business process management news)

4. updates on information systems research (search for: information system news)

5. new software and information systems used in human resources (search for: HRIS software)

6. recent models created using 3-D visualization (search for: 3D visualization)

7. popular quality control programs (search for: latest quality control software)

8. latest online transaction processing applications (search for: online transaction processing news)

9. top content management systems (search for: best content management systems)

10. latest predictions on the future of cloud computing (search for: trends cloud computing)

11. widely used enterprise hardware (search for: enterprise hardware storage)

12. updates on backup and recovery methods (search for: backup recovery procedures news)

13. new real-life neural network uses (search for: neural networks applications)

14. latest news about IBM enterprise technology (search for: IBM enterprise systems)

15. popular consumer electronics devices for the home (search for: new consumer electronics home)

For current news and information
Check us out on Facebook and Twitter. See your instructor or the Computer Concepts CourseMate for specific information.

Quick Reference

Every chapter in this Student Success Guide presents tables of resources targeted toward one of five student goals: informed digital consumer; productive technology user; safe user, protected from the risks in a digital world; competent digital citizen; and future entrepreneur or professional in a digital society. Resources may be located in the textbook, on the Computer Concepts CourseMate Web site, in the Interactive eBook, and on the Web.

Some of the tables throughout the Student Success Guide identify text and/or a figure(s) as the resource, which you will find self-explanatory. For those resources that are not identified as text or figures, the following table provides a quick reference to help you locate each type of resource. The first and second columns name and briefly describe the resource and its purpose. The third column identifies where you can find the resource and, in brackets, outlines how to navigate to resources on the Computer Concepts CourseMate Web site (www.cengagebrain.com). For more detailed instructions about the Computer Concepts CourseMate, refer to the pages specified in the fourth column.

Resource	Purpose	Location [Navigation]	Additional Information
Animations	Strengthen your understanding of chapter topics through animations that correspond directly to book content	Interactive eBook	• 1 per chapter For further instruction, see page 77 in CourseMate Student Guide
		CourseMate [eBook Interactive Activities link on navigation menu | Animations tab]	For further instruction, see page 77 in CourseMate Student Guide
Companies on the Cutting Edge	Expose you to companies you should know in the computer industry	Last page in chapter before Student Assignments	• 2 per chapter
		CourseMate [Beyond the Book link on navigation menu | Beyond the Book tab]	For further instruction, see page 84 in CourseMate Student Guide
Computer Usage @ Work	Familiarize you with ways various industries use computers and related technology	Follows Chapter Summary	• 1 per chapter
		External links with more information on **CourseMate** [Beyond the Book link on navigation menu | Beyond the Book tab]	For further instruction, see page 84 in CourseMate Student Guide
Drag and Drop Figures	Boost your understanding of chapter visuals through interactive figure activities	Interactive eBook	For further instruction, see page 77 in CourseMate Student Guide
		CourseMate [eBook Interactive Activities link on navigation menu | Drag and Drop Figures tab]	For further instruction, see page 77 in CourseMate Student Guide
Ethics & Issues	Heighten your awareness of ethical and controversial computer-related issues	Boxes throughout textbook	• 2 to 4 per chapter • For complete list of topics, see page xii in textbook
		CourseMate [Beyond the Book link on navigation menu | Ethics & Issues tab]	For further instruction, see page 84 in CourseMate Student Guide
Exploring Computer Careers	Familiarize you with various professions in the computer industry	**CourseMate** [Activities and Tutorials link on navigation menu | Exploring Computer Careers tab]	For further instruction, see page 77 in CourseMate Student Guide
FAQs	Ask and answer intriguing or current event questions related to technology	Boxes throughout textbook	• 3 to 5 per chapter • For complete list of topics, see page xii in textbook
		External links with more information on **CourseMate** [Beyond the Book link on navigation menu I Beyond the Book tab]	For further instruction, see page 84 in CourseMate Student Guide

Continued on next page

Continued from previous page

Innovative Computing	Explore original or creative uses of technology to solve traditional problems	Boxes throughout textbook	• 1 per chapter • For complete list of topics, see page xii in textbook
		External links with more information on **CourseMate** [Beyond the Book link on navigation menu | Beyond the Book tab]	For further instruction, see page 84 in CourseMate Student Guide
Labs (Student Edition Labs)	Reinforce and expand your knowledge about basic computer topics	**CourseMate** [Student Edition Labs link on navigation menu]	For further instruction, see page 80 in CourseMate Student Guide
Learn How To	Learn fundamental technology skills for practical everyday tasks through hands-on activities and exercises	Student Assignments in textbook	• 1 to 2 per chapter
		CourseMate [Video Study Tools link on navigation menu | Learn How To tab]	For further instruction, see page 83 in CourseMate Student Guide
Looking Ahead	Alert you to upcoming technological breakthroughs or recent advances in the industry	Boxes throughout textbook	• 1 per chapter • For complete list of topics, see page xiii in textbook
		External links with more information on **CourseMate** [Beyond the Book link on navigation menu | Beyond the Book tab]	For further instruction, see page 84 in CourseMate Student Guide
Technology Trailblazers	Expose you to leaders you should know in the computer industry	Last page in chapter before Student Assignments	• 2 per chapter
		CourseMate [Beyond the Book link on navigation menu | Beyond the Book tab]	For further instruction, see page 84 in CourseMate Student Guide
Videos	Show you current information or varying perspectives through third-party videos	Interactive eBook	For further instruction, see page 77 in CourseMate Student Guide
		CourseMate [eBook Interactive Activities link on navigation menu | Videos tab] **CourseMate** [Video Study Tools link on navigation menu | At the Movies tab]	For further instruction, see page 77 in CourseMate Student Guide For further instruction, see page 83 in CourseMate Student Guide
Web Apps	Learn how to use popular Web apps through practical exercises	**CourseMate** [Activities and Tutorials link on navigation menu | Web Apps tab]	For further instruction, see page 77 in CourseMate Student Guide
Web Links	Present you with current information or varying perspectives through external Web sites	**CourseMate** [Beyond the Book link on navigation menu | Beyond the Book tab]	For further instruction, see page 84 in CourseMate Student Guide
Windows Exercises	Sharpen your Windows skills by stepping through exercises on your computer	**CourseMate** [Activities and Tutorials link on navigation menu | Activities and Tutorials tab]	For further instruction, see page 80 in CourseMate Student Guide

Computer Concepts CourseMate Student Guide

Introduction

Welcome to this Computer Concepts CourseMate Student Guide. Computer Concepts CourseMate is an online collection of tools and resources you can use to enrich the learning process with the *Discovering Computers—Fundamentals: Your Interactive Guide to the Digital World* textbook. This guide will help familiarize you with the navigation of the tools and resources contained in Computer Concepts CourseMate.

To use Computer Concepts CourseMate while following along in this guide, you will need access to:

- A computer
- An Internet connection
- A Web browser

Getting Started on Computer Concepts CourseMate

Computer Concepts CourseMate, which is a Web-based companion to the *Discovering Computers—Fundamentals* textbook, is an easy-to-use and innovative product designed to enhance your learning experience. Access Computer Concepts CourseMate by navigating to http://login.cengagebrain.com in a Web browser. Set up a user name if you do not have one already, log in, and then use the printed access code to register your Computer Concepts CourseMate product.

After successful login to Computer Concepts CourseMate, the My Dashboard page will be displayed (Figure 1). On the My Dashboard page, follow these steps to add the *Discovering Computers—Fundamentals* textbook to your bookshelf:

1. Type the title ISBN, author name, or title in the 'Add a title to your bookshelf' text box.
2. Click the Search button to display the Discovering Computers—Fundamentals product on your bookshelf.

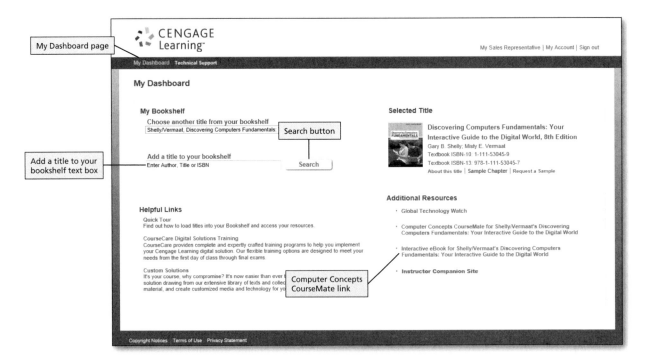

Figure 1

Once the book is added to your bookshelf, its associated Computer Concepts CourseMate link will be listed in the Additional Resources area of this page (shown in Figure 1). Click the Computer Concepts CourseMate link, which in this case, is called Computer Concepts CourseMate for Shelly/Vermaat's Discovering Computers—Fundamentals: Your Interactive Guide to the Digital World, to open the Computer Concepts CourseMate for *Discovering Computers—Fundamentals* (Figure 2).

Figure 2

Using the Interactive eBook

You can access all of the textbook content through Computer Concepts CourseMate's Interactive eBook on your desktop or mobile computer, as long as you have an Internet connection. Open the Interactive eBook by clicking the Chapter eBook link on the navigation menu (shown in Figure 2), which is located on the left side of Computer Concepts CourseMate. The Interactive eBook not only displays all of the information in the text but also includes many interactive tools that are not available in the printed textbook. Figure 3 on the next page identifies specific tools in the Interactive eBook. For a brief description about how to use each of the tools, click the Help button in the upper-right corner of the Interactive eBook.

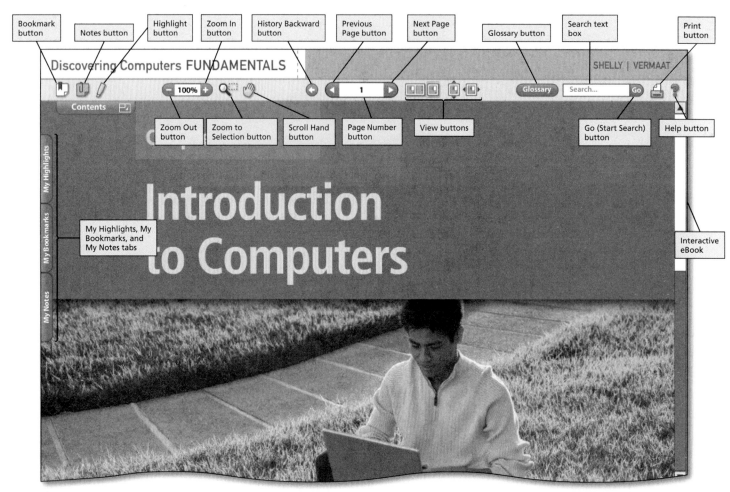

Figure 3

You can browse quickly through pages of text in the Interactive eBook, search for a term, zoom in to a section of a page, view multiple page layouts, take notes on a specific item, highlight text, bookmark a section, or search the glossary for a specific key term by using the buttons identified in Figure 3. To display all of your highlights, bookmarks, or notes, click the respective tabs on the left side of the Interactive eBook; or, you can print your highlights or notes using the Print button in the upper-right corner of the Interactive eBook. To display a different chapter or feature, click the Table of Contents button in the upper-left corner and then click the desired chapter on the menu.

Key terms, which are shaded gray throughout the Interactive eBook for easy identification, are links. Click any key term to display the Mini Glossary, where you can view the definition of the key term, listen to an audio recording of the term, and display external links associated with the term (Figure 4).

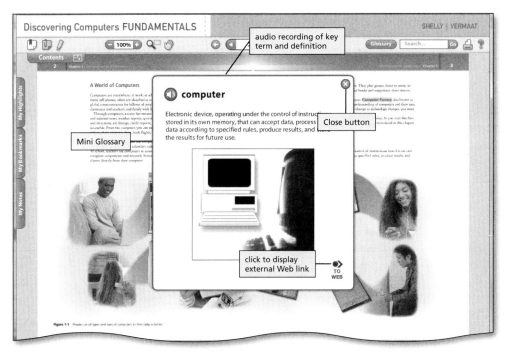

Figure 4

Learning Key Terms and Definitions

Computer Concepts CourseMate includes multiple resources to help you learn the terms and concepts in the *Discovering Computers—Fundamentals* textbook. These resources include Interactive Flashcards, Key Terms, and games.

Instead of using index cards to create your own flashcards, you can use the Interactive Flashcards in Computer Concepts CourseMate to learn, review, and test your knowledge of key terms (Figure 5). These flashcards appear on the screen and look similar to those you would make yourself. While using the Interactive Flashcards, you can choose to display the definition or the term first, shuffle the deck, remove terms, or show all cards. If you simply want a list of the glossary items in one place for quick reference, click the Key Terms link, instead of the Interactive Flashcards link, on the navigation menu on the left side of Computer Concepts CourseMate.

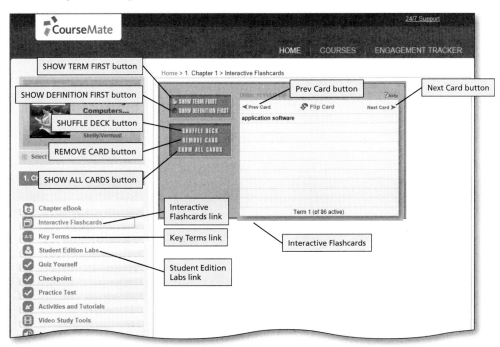

Figure 5

Do you want to challenge your knowledge of chapter content? The Crossword Puzzle resource covers the chapter's key terms and definitions. The Crossword Puzzle is a timed activity, which provides options to check your answers, undo incorrect answers, and submit your final solution. Complete the crossword puzzle to solidify your knowledge of the key terms and their definitions. To access the Crossword Puzzle resource, click the Activities and Tutorials link on the navigation menu on the left side of Computer Concepts CourseMate.

Wheel of Terms is another fun Computer Concepts CourseMate learning tool that tests your key term knowledge (Figure 6). Spin the wheel, pick a letter, buy a vowel, or submit your answer to the definition shown above the board. As you solve the puzzle and earn game money, you also build confidence for an upcoming exam. To access the Wheel of Terms resource, click the Activities and Tutorials link on the navigation menu on the left side of Computer Concepts CourseMate.

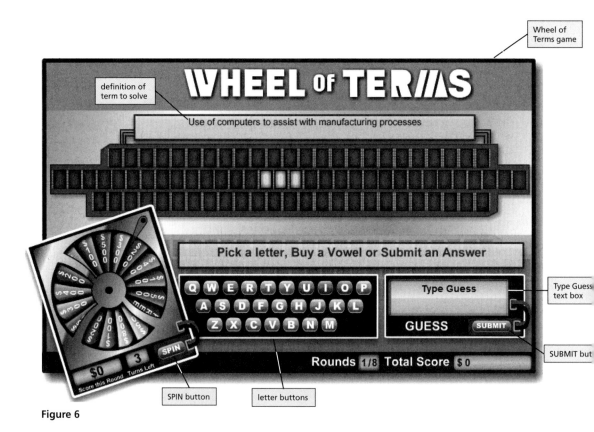

Figure 6

Hands-On Labs and Exercises

Computer Concepts CourseMate includes a variety of hands-on resources so that you can practice items covered in the textbook. Two of these resources are the Student Edition Labs and Windows Exercises.

To display the Student Edition Labs associated with a chapter, click the Student Edition Labs link on the navigation menu, which is located on the left side of Computer Concepts CourseMate (shown in Figure 5 on the previous page). You can start any individual lab in the list by clicking its link and then clicking the Start button for the lab. Figure 7 shows a sample lab and identifies elements of the interface.

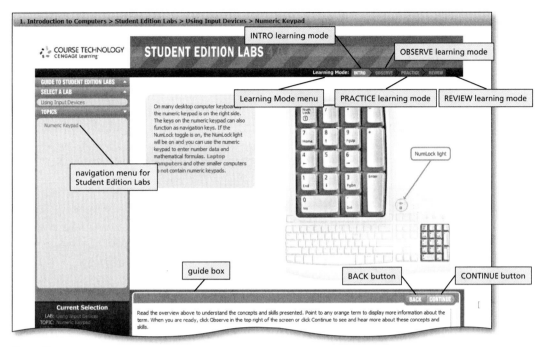

Figure 7

You interact with labs through four learning modes: Intro, Observe, Practice, and Review (shown in Figure 7). Each mode is designed to provide a cohesive path to learning the task. The Intro learning mode presents an overview of the topic; the Observe learning mode provides audio and visual guides; the Practice learning mode offers step-by-step instructions; and the Review learning mode supplies a series of multiple choice questions. At the bottom of each learning mode screen is a guide box that contains instructions for completing the lab and buttons for navigating through the lab.

Each Computer Concepts CourseMate chapter offers several Windows Exercises tailored to accompany the textbook and expand your knowledge of Windows. These step-by-step exercises vary by chapter and should be performed on a local computer. To access the Windows Exercises, click the Activities and Tutorials link on the navigation menu on the left side of the Computer Concepts CourseMate and then click the desired Windows Exercise.

Comprehensive Test Preparation

Computer Concepts CourseMate not only supplies resources to help you learn the chapter content, it also can help prepare you for quizzes and tests. Gauge your knowledge before a chapter exam using these resources: Computer Genius, Quiz Yourself, Checkpoint, You're Hired!, and Practice Test.

Who wants to be a Computer Genius? Are you ready to test your knowledge? Computer Genius tests your knowledge of the chapter content in a game-show environment. Start the Computer Genius game by clicking the Activities and Tutorials link on the Computer Concepts CourseMate navigation menu and then clicking the Computer Genius link. Computer Genius is a timed, multiple choice quiz that will test your knowledge of important concepts, terms, and ideas in the chapter text. If you are stumped on a question, use the Panic Buttons, such as the Book, 50/50, Survey, Double-Dip, and 3 Professors, before submitting your final answer.

Are you ready to look for a job? The You're Hired! game tests your understanding of chapter key terms in an interactive, timed simulation. In this simulation, you answer questions based on chapter content at a career fair, in an internship, and then in a job interview, to prove you are the right person for the job. If you answer questions incorrectly, the You're Hired! game allows you to repeat the level or to print a study guide to refine your answers for the time you play. To access You're Hired!, click the Activities and Tutorials link on the Computer Concepts CourseMate navigation menu and then click the You're Hired! link.

Prepare for your next quiz using the Quiz Yourself resource. The quizzes are grouped by chapter objectives. To begin a quiz, click the Quiz Yourself link on the Computer Concepts CourseMate navigation menu, click the desired objective groups on the Objectives tabs at the top of the screen, read the instructions, and then click the Start button. When you are finished taking the quiz, click the Done button and review your score and results. Results on the Quiz Summary screen are cross-referenced with the textbook and the Interactive eBook. If you have an incorrect answer, you can click the magnifying glass icon to the right of the answer to display the location of the correct answer in the textbook and the Interactive eBook (Figure 8).

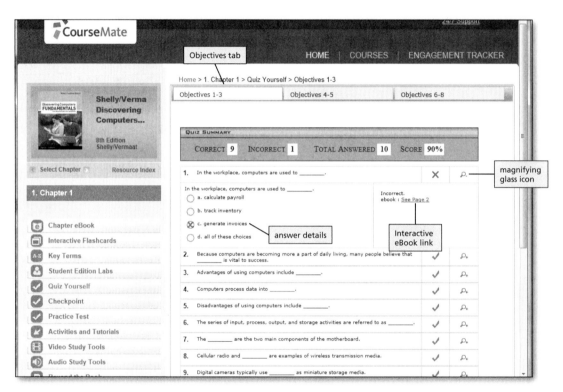

Figure 8

The Checkpoint resource checks your key term and chapter knowledge using matching, true/false, and multiple choice questions. When you click the Checkpoint link on the Computer Concepts CourseMate navigation menu, the first screen displays the Matching activity; to switch to True/False or Multiple Choice, click the desired name on the Checkpoint tabs at the top of the screen. Begin any of the activities by clicking the Start button. When you are finished with the activity, click the Done button, and review your results. Like the Quiz Yourself activity, you can cross-reference your responses using the magnifying glass icon.

The Practice Test is the most comprehensive tool to test your chapter knowledge (Figure 9). Because the Practice Test simulates a real test, it is an extremely important resource on Computer Concepts CourseMate. Click the Practice Test link on the Computer Concepts CourseMate navigation menu to begin the test. As with the other quizzes on Computer Concepts CourseMate, all answers are verified and your score appears after you click the Done button. All answers include a magnifying glass icon, which, when clicked, provides a cross-reference to the textbook and the Interactive eBook. In preparation for the best results on the real exam, try to achieve a 100 percent score on the Practice Test.

Figure 9

Enhanced Study Aids

Computer Concepts CourseMate includes both audio and video tools to further enhance your learning experience with the *Discovering Computers—Fundamentals* textbook. The Video Study Tools, accessed from the Computer Concepts CourseMate navigation menu by clicking the Video Study Tools link, include these tools: You Review It, At the Movies, Learn How To, and Quiz: Learn How To. To use a particular tool, click its name on the Video Study Tools tabs at the top of the screen. The first three tools use videos, podcasts, or vodcasts of content related to the textbook; the Learn How To Quiz tests your knowledge of the material in the Learn How To video resource.

Sometimes, if you listen to text being read, you might absorb it into memory better than if you read it. For this reason, Computer Concepts CourseMate provides audio files of key terms and chapter content. To access these audio files, click the Audio Study Tools link on the Computer Concepts CourseMate navigation menu (Figure 10 on the next page). Audio tools are available for both the Chapter Review and the chapter key terms. Access each by clicking the respective resource name on the Audio Study Tools tabs at the top of the screen. Read the on-screen instructions, then download the audio files to a local computer or preferred portable media player, so that you can listen to the audio files offline.

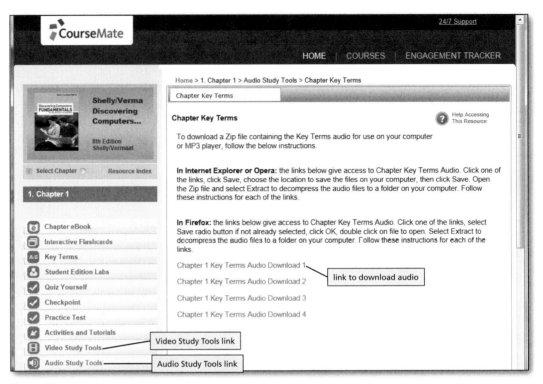

Figure 10

Explore Other Resources

Your *Discovering Computers—Fundamentals* textbook presents a great wealth of information; Computer Concepts CourseMate expands on this information with the Beyond the Book and Ethics & Issues resources. Click the Beyond the Book link on the Computer Concepts CourseMate navigation menu to display a host of external links that are referenced throughout the chapter text. Click any link to explore resources outside of the Computer Concepts CourseMate interface. If you click Ethics & Issues on the Beyond the Book tabs at the top of the screen, text from all of the Ethics & Issues boxes in the chapter will be displayed in one convenient location. Learn, explore, and provide answers to various ethical questions pertaining to chapter topics.

Book-Level Resources at the bottom of the Computer Concepts CourseMate navigation menu include the following: Install Computer, Maintain Computer, Timeline, Buyer's Guide, Digital Forensics, Making Use of the Web, and Global Technology Watch (Figure 11). Each of these tools is designed to enhance your *Discovering Computers—Fundamentals* experience by providing additional information or external, third-party links.

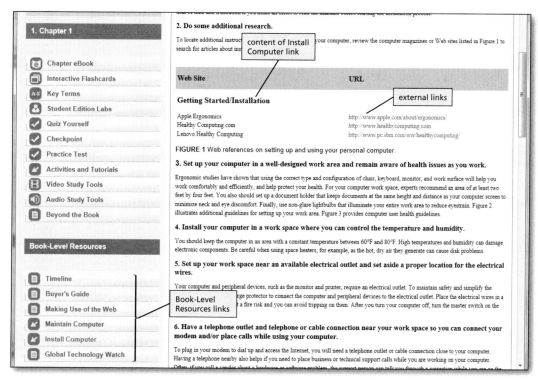

Figure 11

New Web Apps

New to Computer Concepts CourseMate for *Discovering Computers—Fundamentals* are three Web applications (Web apps) that aid student comprehension of chapter material. These Web apps are available only via Computer Concepts CourseMate and are developed for use on smart phones, as well as on tablets, notebook computers, and desktop computers.

Improve retention of the chapter key terms with the Flashcard Web app. Study for an exam by reviewing major points in each chapter with the Study Guide Web app or with the Practice Test Web app that provides multiple choice questions.

Use the new Web apps as part of your overall *Discovering Computers—Fundamentals* learning experience to help you succeed using *Discovering Computers—Fundamentals*.

Summary

Computer Concepts CourseMate is designed for use as a companion to the *Discovering Computers— Fundamentals: Your Interactive Guide to the Digital World* textbook. Conveniently organized in one location, all of the tools and resources in Computer Concepts CourseMate will help you learn. You can leave your book at home and use the Interactive eBook, study key terms, work on a simulated lab or explore other activities, download audio of key terms, watch a video related to the chapter text, take a practice quiz or exam, extend your learning experience outside of the book with external resources, and much more! Computer Concepts CourseMate is designed carefully to help you succeed using *Discovering Computers—Fundamentals*.

WebTutor Student Guide

Objectives

You will have mastered the material in this guide when you can:

- Log in to Angel and Blackboard to access WebTutor content
- View Topic Reviews, PowerPoint Presentations, Practice Tests, and Topic Review Questions in Course Documents
- View Assignments
- Access and complete Assessments and Activities

Introduction

Welcome to the Discovering Computers—Fundamentals 2012 Student Guide to WebTutor. The purpose of this guide is to orient you to the WebTutor online tools, which supplement the *Discovering Computers—Fundamentals: Your Interactive Guide to the Digital World* textbook. The WebTutor online materials will assist you with interactive ways of learning the material in your textbook.

Log in to Angel or Blackboard

You can access WebTutor via the Web applications Angel or Blackboard. In this section, you will log in to each of these applications.

Access WebTutor in Angel

Log in to Angel The following steps log in to Angel to access WebTutor.

- Start a Web browser, navigate to your school's Angel site, and then log in.
- Click the Discovering Computers—Fundamentals ©2012 title in the Courses list to display information for the course in which you are enrolled (Figure 1).

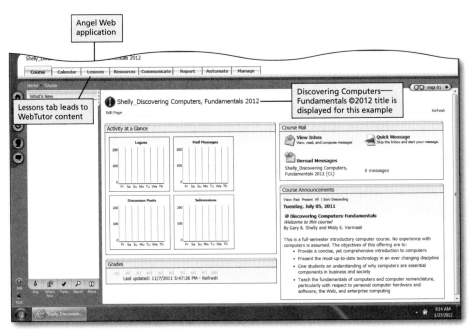

Figure 1

Access WebTutor in Blackboard

Log in to Blackboard The following steps log in to Blackboard to access WebTutor.

- Start a Web browser, navigate to your school's Blackboard site, and then log in.

- Click the Courses tab, if necessary, to view the course list.

- Click the appropriate Discovering Computers— Fundamentals ©2012 title in the course list to display information for the course in which you are enrolled (Figure 2).

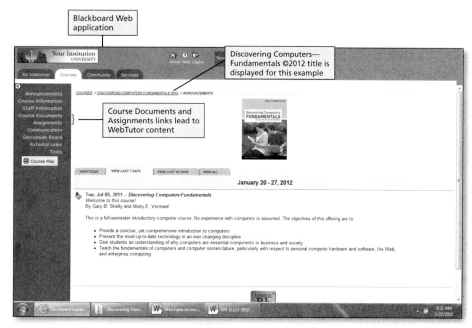

Figure 2

Course Documents

WebTutor contains course documents that reinforce the textbook content. The types of course documents are Topic Review, PowerPoint Presentations, Practice Test, and Topic Review Questions. In order to access course documents, log in to a WebTutor application (Angel or Blackboard) and then navigate to the course documents. Within the course documents are links to each chapter of the textbook. Click a chapter's link to display the list of WebTutor course documents for that chapter.

Topic Review

The WebTutor Topic Review is a course document that corresponds to the textbook's Chapter Review, which is located in the Student Assignments section of each chapter. Figure 3 shows a sample WebTutor Topic Review course document in Angel and Blackboard. Each link in the Topic Review corresponds to one of the statements or questions in bold in the textbook's Chapter Review. After thinking about the instruction and your response, click the corresponding link to view the answer, which also is located in the Chapter Review in the textbook. Table 1 shows the click path to the WebTutor Topic Review in each application.

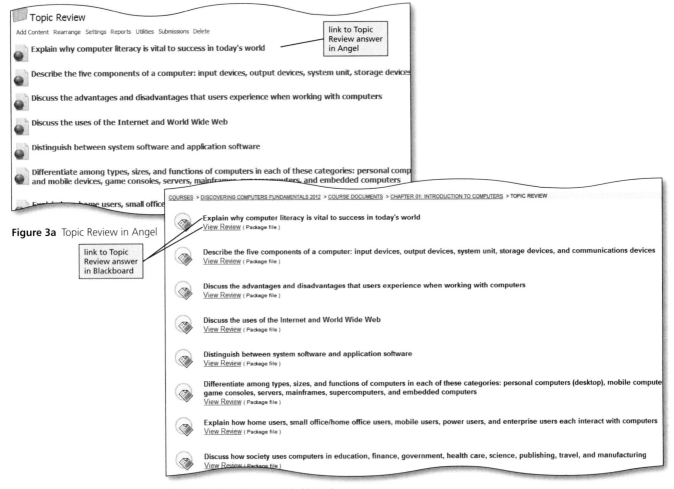

Figure 3a Topic Review in Angel

Figure 3b Topic Review in Blackboard

Figure 3

Table 1 Topic Review Click Path (substitute the chapter number in place of the * in the path)	
WEB APPLICATION	PATH
Angel	Lessons tab > Course Documents > Chapter * > Topic Review
Blackboard	Courses tab > Course Documents > Chapter * > Topic Review

PowerPoint Presentations

WebTutor contains PowerPoint presentations to reinforce the textbook content. Each PowerPoint presentation shows a high-level overview of the textbook chapter's contents. The presentations begin with the same image contained on the textbook chapter's first page, and the slides highlight key terms and figures in the chapter. The slides also contain graphical representations of lists of important information to remember. For example, Figure 4 shows slides from the presentation for Chapter 1 of the Discovering Computers—Fundamentals 2012 textbook. On the PowerPoint Presentations in each WebTutor application, you either can view a presentation online in a browser or download the presentation. Table 2 shows the click path to the WebTutor PowerPoint Presentations in each application.

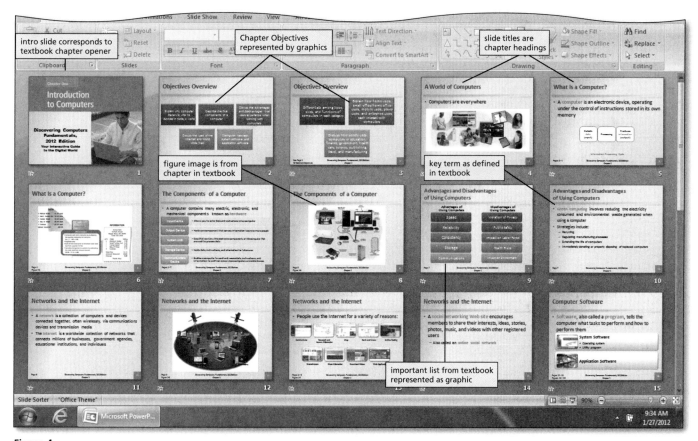

Figure 4

Table 2 PowerPoint Presentations Click Path (substitute the chapter number in place of the * in the path)	
WEB APPLICATION	**PATH**
Angel	Lessons tab > Course Documents > Chapter * > PowerPoint Presentations
Blackboard	Courses tab > Course Documents > Chapter * > PowerPoint Presentations

Practice Test

The WebTutor Practice Test is a course document that presents an extensive online test, which you can use to practice answering questions about the material covered in a chapter (Figure 5). Because the Practice Test is not printed in the textbook, you will find this tool useful in studying for your exams. The content for the questions is taken from the textbook and will reinforce the information. Also, practicing answering the questions will help prepare you for answering exam questions.

When you have completed a Practice Test, you can submit it for a grade. If desired, you can retake the test to improve your grade; only the latest grade is recorded in the online grade book. The test likely will include multiple choice, true/false, completion, matching, and/or essay questions. Table 3 shows the click path to the WebTutor Practice Test in each application.

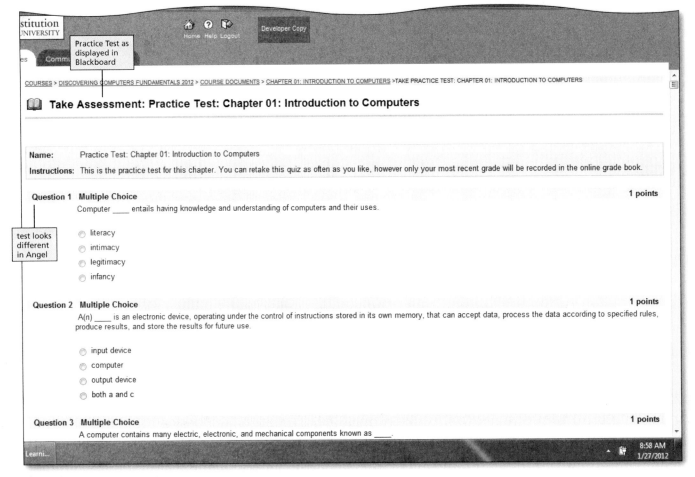

Figure 5

Table 3 Practice Test Click Path (substitute the chapter number in place of the * in the path)	
WEB APPLICATION	PATH
Angel	Lessons tab > Quizzes > Practice Test: Chapter *
	Lessons tab > Question Banks > Practice Test: Chapter *
Blackboard	Courses tab > Course Documents > Chapter * > Practice Test

Topic Review Questions

The Topic Review Questions are an abbreviated version of the Practice Tests that you can use to practice answering possible test questions about the material covered in the chapter (Figure 6). Like the Practice Test, the Topic Review Questions are not located in the textbook. Topic Review Questions can be used as a quick self-assessment tool to gauge how well you know the textbook chapter's material. As with the Practice Test, practicing answering the questions will help prepare you for answering exam questions.

After completing the quiz, you can submit it for a grade. If desired, you can retake the quiz to improve your grade; only the latest grade is recorded in the online grade book. This short quiz could include true/false, multiple choice, and completion questions. Table 4 shows the click path to the WebTutor Topic Review Questions in each application.

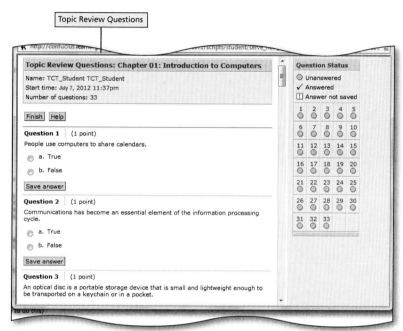

Figure 6

Table 4 **Topic Review Questions Click Path**	
(substitute the chapter number in place of the * in the path)	
WEB APPLICATION	PATH
Angel	Lessons tab > Quizzes > Topic Review Questions: Chapter *
	Lessons tab > Question Banks > Topic Review Questions: Chapter *
Blackboard	Courses tab > Course Documents > Chapter * > Topic Review Questions

Assignments

Assignments in WebTutor are additional materials designed to enhance your understanding of the information in the textbook. The content of the assignments varies by title and chapter and includes an assignment topic that links to a suggested exercise (Figure 7a). When you click a link, the suggested exercise will appear (Figure 7b). Your instructor may assign the essay to you, or you may choose to complete an assignment to better understand topics in the textbook. Table 5 shows the click path to the WebTutor Assignments in each application.

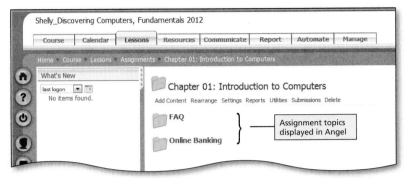

Figure 7a Assignment Topics

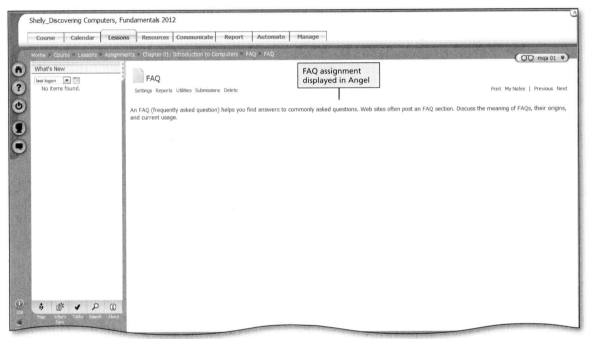

Figure 7b FAQ Assignment

Figure 7

Table 5 **Assignments Click Path** (substitute the chapter number in place of the * in the path)	
WEB APPLICATION	PATH
Angel	Lessons tab > Assignments > Chapter *
Blackboard	Courses tab > Assignments > Chapter *

Summary

The WebTutor online course documents — Topic Reviews, PowerPoint Presentations, Practice Tests, and Topic Review Questions, and Assignments — reinforce the information in the Discovering Computers—Fundamentals ©2012 textbook. You can access the WebTutor online tools using the Angel or Blackboard Web applications.